Mall Walking in San Diego County

by
William Carroll

First Edition

Printed in the United States of America

ISBN 0-910390-31-2

Library of Congress Catalog Card Number: 90-86355

Coda Publications
P.O. Bin 711
San Marcos, California 92079-0711

For Skip, with my grateful appreciation.

W.C.

Contents

"We all grow older but we do not have to become old"

The Singles' Philosopher

Mall Walking in San Diego County

There are more than 100 malls and shopping centers in San Diego County that have walking space for everyone with time to enjoy better health. Mall walking, which for Southern Californians includes shopping-center walking, adds only a few minutes to the grocery-buying routine and can make the difference between leading a sedentary existence or living with buoyant energy that has been untapped since the last time you went for a walk.

Mall Walking in San Diego County lists hundreds of typical walks both in and around area malls and shopping centers. These walks have all been measured and range from 2/10th-mile (.2) strolls along the sidewalk in front of the stores to multi-mile constitutionals around the perimeter of the entire complex. In addition, where appropriate, longer walks have been routed through the neighborhood adjoining the mall or shopping center.

Walking sites are alphabetized in this book by the city or community area in which they are located, then by the common name of the complex. Each listing includes the center's address, city and zip code. *The Thomas Guide* of street maps for San Diego and Imperial County is used to provide the walking site's specific page and grid location on street maps of the site area. In addition, there are references to street intersection location, parking entry streets and source of public transit services or transportation schedule information. Final pages of *Mall Walking in San Diego County* contain a cross-index to first find a walking site by the common name of the complex and then be directed to it's page number.

Mall Walking in San Diego County

We define a "Mall" as an enclosed climate-controlled structure containing a great variety of retail stores and consumer services. Malls are suitable for walking during any season of the year. Mornings are best as there are fewer shoppers in the hallways to interfere with fast walking.

A "large" shopping center often occupies many acres. It will have one or more major department stores, food chain outlets and an extensive collection of boutique and community service retailers. In addition to fast food and delicatessens, you will often find a variety of moderate-price restaurants.

A "medium" size shopping center may occupy all or most of a city block, It usually provides one or more fast-food franchises, a restaurant and a wide selection of community service retailers. Food chains, a major drug or small department store and building supply concern are often represented.

A "small" shopping center is usually an L-shaped complex of community stores in one corner of a block of residential housing. Many have delicatessens or small cafes for food service. The anchor store is often a food chain outlet.

The primary photograph of each walking site shows the entry drive or most obvious identification sign. In a few instances no sign is used and an overall view of the site has been substituted. Site maps of malls and two speciality centers show the suggested measured walks.

Genuine honest-to-goodness enclosed malls are few in San Diego County because their air-conditioned environment is seldom needed with our mediterranean-style Southern California climate. These covered malls in San Diego are delightful places for walking ventures and can be held in reserve for exercise on days when gusty winds or rain make the outerworld uncomfortable. In addition; in the Malls section you will find several unusual shopping centers which have been included because of their substantial differences from the typical Southern California community shopping complex.

Accordingly the majority of the listed walking sites are shopping centers ranging from enormous complexes covering many acres to tiny neighborhood service facilities tucked into a portion of a city block. Most offer enchanting opportunities for neighborhood walks. A large enclosed mall in Imperial County has been listed for readers who would like to combine viewing the spectacular Borrego Desert with a trip to nearby El Centro for mall walking. Adjoining San Diego County on the north is the "Old West" theme town of Temecula which has a modern walking area of interest. Unfortunately it is about one mile from the town center of historic buildings and antique shops.

Most malls and shopping centers are located in community areas served by public transportation. Those complexes midway between the City of San Diego and what is termed North County are usually blessed with two public transportation systems: One from the south, another from the north.

Visitors to enclosed malls will find that restroom facilities are mapped on a Directory Board located near the main entrance or in the central foyer of the hallways. Finding the restrooms may be a little difficult as most do not have large identification signs. Inquire with merchants in the general area for specific directions. All restrooms were found to be spotlessly clean and fully serviced with supplies. Open shopping centers with strips of individual stores are not required to provide such facilities. Those few that do maintain public restrooms are identified in their individual listings on Pages 28 to 132. Car parks which surround larger malls and shopping centers are usually monitored by mobile security patrols.

Food is the last problem anyone has while mall or shopping-center walking. You will find everything from the most popular fast-food franchises to well-known upscale restaurants with ocean views and expensive menus. Perhaps the major concern would be finding a diet-light meal. However; with a few extra miles of walking one could enjoy both the meal and pleasure of walking off added pounds from high-calorie entrees.

For malls, a site map has been included to show walking routes and distances. For both malls and shopping centers; reference material on each page provides a general description of services available and typical business hours for major retailers. Additional notations define the availability of public rest rooms, benches, restaurants and security patrols in the shopping area and parking lots.

Within *Mall Walking in San Diego County* you will discover many new walking sites worth visiting. There is specific information on how to get there, what you will find on arrival, and pre-measured walks making it easy to keep track of how much exercise you accomplish during each walking venture.

Walking and Health

Walking for better health is like motherhood and apple pie. Most of us find it hard to argue against such good old-fashion values. Or disagree with more than one million people who are reported to be walking for health through malls or shopping centers any one day of the week.

Techniques are simple, the cost low and opportunities everywhere. More so now than in days past when recreational walking was thought of as requiring a costly and time-consuming trip to the country. Most San Diego County shopping centers and malls are suitable for beneficial exercise and within easy reach by public transportation or private car. Because food services are readily available, there's no need to pack a lunch nor any valid excuse not to consider regular walking ventures as an aid to creating a more fruitful lifestyle.

A good level of health-supporting activity is said to be about 30 minutes of moderately fast walking four times a week. Should you be overweight, walk for a longer period of time and eat less until the weight problem is minimal and your body chemistry becomes balanced. Medical reports indicate that a body in good condition does a better job of using its food intake than a body in poor condition. This is another way of saying a healthy body gains less from the same meal that would add un-wanted pounds onto a body less functional.

It was also reported that about three months of consistent vigorous exercise will bring almost any useful body up to its reasonable peak. Certainly you can work out in a gym or health spa and build muscles, jog or run and build wind, lift weights and improve what you are able to raise off the ground; but these are add-ons to being healthy. In the beginning; the values of feeling better and being more in control are initial, and the most important, benefits of simply walking for health.

It is worth pointing out that if you plan any walking venture to be a vigorous workout, begin with five or ten minutes of slow walking to give the body time to warm up to its new task.

Once warmed up, consider walking a mile in about 12 minutes. This equals five miles an hour and is a very fast walk. A moderate pace would be a mile in about 15 minutes which is four miles an hour. The secret to making either speed a maximum-effort walk is a full swing of the arms with every step. In effect this adds upper body exercise to benefits usually reserved for legs, lungs and heart. The arm waving technique should be practiced for short distances over a period of several days while building up to its use for the full mile. You may meet walkers who have added one or two weights to their wrists, or carry plastic containers of water in each hand, as additions to the workout factor. It is estimated they gain four or five percent more benefit from their workout by adding such weight. A similar advantage could be achieved by walking five percent further and leaving the accessories at home.

Shoe selection for walking lends itself to more questions than ordering dinner in a foreign country where one does not speak the language. The most important factor of a well-fitting shoe is that it be comfortable to the entire foot. Secondly, buy only a shoe designed for walking; which running, jogging, tennis and basketball shoes are not.

A top-quality shoe similar to that shown on the next page will be less expensive in the long run and provide maximum comfort for your hard-working feet. There's little problem finding the proper last for it is said there are over 200 different models available. Some manufacturers can fit walkers from AAAA to EE, in sizes 4 to 14, men's and women's. Once past the size problem, look for a flexible shoe with fabric uppers that breathe easily and allow your feet to perspire without drowning. For mall or shopping center walking you need a well cushioned outer and inner sole to protect delicate foot bones from the constant pounding on smooth pavement. The soft outer sole should have a number of narrow grooves to give good traction on smooth or wet surfaces. If you have a tendency to wear a shoe's sole off to one side or the other, consider ankle-high tops to support your ankles and straighten your walk.

Mall Walking in San Diego County

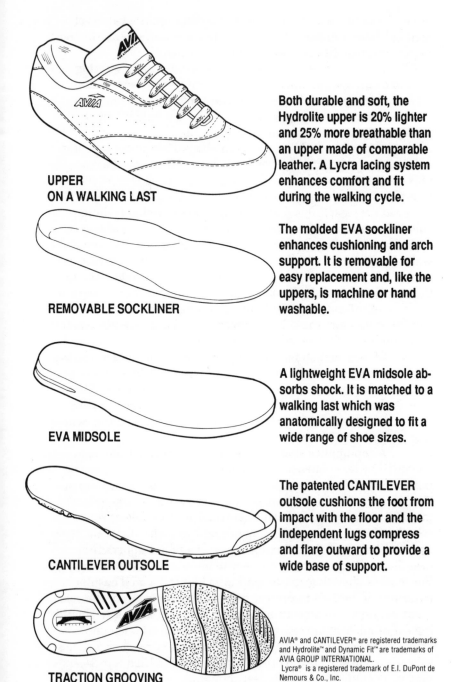

**UPPER
ON A WALKING LAST**

Both durable and soft, the Hydrolite upper is 20% lighter and 25% more breathable than an upper made of comparable leather. A Lycra lacing system enhances comfort and fit during the walking cycle.

REMOVABLE SOCKLINER

The molded EVA sockliner enhances cushioning and arch support. It is removable for easy replacement and, like the uppers, is machine or hand washable.

EVA MIDSOLE

A lightweight EVA midsole absorbs shock. It is matched to a walking last which was anatomically designed to fit a wide range of shoe sizes.

CANTILEVER OUTSOLE

The patented CANTILEVER outsole cushions the foot from impact with the floor and the independent lugs compress and flare outward to provide a wide base of support.

TRACTION GROOVING

AVIA® and CANTILEVER® are registered trademarks and Hydrolite™ and Dynamic Fit™ are trademarks of AVIA GROUP INTERNATIONAL.
 Lycra® is a registered trademark of E.I. DuPont de Nemours & Co., Inc.

Mall Walking in San Diego County

Keep in mind that while high shoes offer better support, they are heavier; about which more later. Low shoes may be easier to walk in but provide the least support. A good compromise is the well-designed shoe with a collar which fits snugly below the ankle and is sufficiently flexible to be comfortable.

For sure; bring or buy a pair of thick walking socks to wear while trying on new shoes: Otherwise you could end up with shoes that will be much too tight when put to hard use. The shape of the sole should match your foot. When standing in the laced shoe, insist on from 1/3rd to 1/2-inch of space between your big toe and end of the shoe. If the area over the toe is high, and there is plenty of room between your toenail and interior of the shoe, that is a plus. A padded roll around the top with an extension pad up the back, which is called a scree collar, can be good or bad depending on fit of the shoe and what feels most comfortable to you. A well-fitting upper must lace to a snug fit around the entire foot to keep it from sliding inside the shoe and wearing blisters as you walk.

An informative test is to walk fast and hard in the shoes you are planning to buy. This is the only way you can be sure their areas of flexibility and stiffness are harmonious with the manner in which your feet are used to working. The best walking shoes have what is called a "power sole" to help you stride easily. They roll naturally forward from the moment you plant your heel until you move forward and lift the toe area to take another step. Poor shoes could be painful and may inhibit every step.

Two final points to consider: One is shoe weight. You will pick them up and lay them down many thousands of times during a day's walk. The less they weigh the easier walking is. On the other hand a heavy shoe gives your muscles more of a workout. Leather walkers usually weigh more than shoes made with uppers of synthetic breathable fabrics.

The second point is flexibility. A soft shoe that is too flexible provides little assistance to control your stride. A stiff shoe provides extra stride control but may feel like a Dutch wooden clog. Try for the comfortable balance between soft and firm that makes you feel most secure while walking over a variety of hard paved surfaces: Such as stairs, escalators, grids, smooth concrete, rough asphalt or pebbled non-skid areas.

Walking inside a mall with its controlled equitable climate, or around shopping centers in most Southern California seasons, calls for the least possible investment in clothing. Underwear is best when made from polyester or polypropylene. These man-made fabrics allow natural body moisture to pass through and evaporate which helps keep your body at its normal temperature. Cotton is comfortable but tends to hold moisture and become soggy. Outerwear could be a simple sweat suit to keep you as warm as you like or loose fitting tropical clothing if you enjoy being a bit on the cool side. A light jacket would be a colorful identifier and enough protection for the final walk to the car park after you're finished. However, if you have to wait outside in the cold for public transportation, be sure to have an insulated outer jacket and head covering to keep from chilling. A hat can be worn and the jacket carried while mall walking.

Should you be exercising outside a shopping center during inclement weather, the more closely you maintain a normal body temperature the better you will feel. Wear good quality thermal underwear made of a synthetic fabric to pass and evaporate body moisture. Pants, shirts and sweaters should maintain warmth and be worn in layers as the temperature dictates. A good jacket with a weatherproof nylon outer surface over its inside lining of fleece or wool is desirable. You will find a headcovering welcome on a rainy day, during one of Southern California's infrequent wind storms or when the sun is skin-burning hot. Double socks, thin pair inside, thick outside, do a good job or preventing blisters. In short, be comfortable.

Eating is seldom a bad idea and current opinions suggest that four light meals a day are best of all. Plan ahead to maintain your energy at a useful level instead of creating the highs and lows associated with heavy spread-out meals. A light breakfast when you walk early will allow brunching at ten or eleven. Or brunch first, then walk the noon hours away. Break longer mall or shopping center ventures with an iced tea or lemonade stop, to rest the body and replace lost fluids. If you snack while exercising select carbohydrates and leave fatty, protein-rich, meals for social events and appreciation of mother's home cooking. One bit of good diet news which surfaced from a recent research project was a report indicating that mild exercise, like walking, greatly improved the body's beneficial use of protein. In effect, with regular exercise you may be able to enjoy a greater variety of tasty foods with less damage to your vitality.

When possible, schedule your walking with a partner or group. Comparisons and challenges will add pleasure to the venture because friends will often cause you to exercise a bit harder than you might push by yourself. All of which adds up to greater measures of improvement to overall health.

As you walk with others you will notice as many postures as there are walkers. How you upgrade your body could begin with standing comfortably erect to raise the rib cage and give your lungs the maximum amount of space within which to expand. Then maintain your shoulders back and level by noting where the thumbs touch your thighs. Unless your arms are grossly unequal, the thumbs should be in about the same place on each side. A further improvement in posture will come from pulling your stomach in and thrusting the hip joints forward to set the spine in a near vertical position. This tends to eliminate the "swayback" posture which causes so many complaints of aching back.

Swing your arms naturally and use a normal length step while warming up. After the five minute warm-up, begin swinging your legs forward and striding out as far as is comfortable. This striding-out technique exercises muscles with a bit of gentle stretching. It also allows the hip joints a chance to explore new territory and reduce their aches and pains from the stiffness of inaction. Move each foot well out, put it down on the heel, roll the foot forward and pick up cleanly. Practice an aggressive walking technique with the same attention you would give the game of golf. Then, when postured walking becomes so natural you no longer think about it, take a good look at yourself in a store window as you stride past. The new image of a healthy well-figured person will be all the reward you will need.

There appears to be very little difference between benefits from mall and shopping-center walking as compared to operating a treadmill or stair-step device. It simply boils down to how long you walk, whether it is uphill or down, and slow or fast: Plus how convenient it is to exercise when and where.

According to the *Wellness Letter*, published by the University of California in Berkeley, being continually active is the key to weight control and good health for an average person. Burning 1000 calories a week in moderate activity is the *Letter's* basic recommendation for health-giving exercise. Normal health being considered, age appears to be of little importance. Reasonable activity has been shown to improve mobility and strength for individuals 80 and 90 years of age. Neck stiffness, back pain and headaches have long been known to become less a problem during and following regular exercise programs. A reduction of stress and improved cardio-vascular performance are believed to be responsible for the decrease in such painful common problems.

Not to mention that regular exercise has long been known to help us all live better and enjoy more.

Which is what walking is all about: Living better. No matter where you are in San Diego County there is a mall or shopping complex nearby. Next time combine your usual visit to the food store with a bit of exercise. It will feel so good that a regular schedule, like 30 minutes of medium speed walking four times a week, may be easy to establish. From then on it's all for the good: Fewer problems with weight control, better general health, and more new friends with similar objectives.

Walking for health is today's way to go.

How Each Walking Site Is Described

Location   **Mall or Shopping Center**
Where it is.   The most commonly used name.

Description: The size of site and what is generally available.
Located at: The street address, City and Zip Code.
Community/Area name: The name by which the area is known.
Thomas Guide: Page, Grid. (Where you will find this site
    in the *Thomas Guide* of maps to San Diego County.)
Intersection of: Major cross streets nearest the site.
Transit service: The transit company and bus number(s).
    CVT = Chula Vista Transit   476-9914.
    CTS = County Transit System   233-3004.
    ECT = El Centro Transit   353-3520.
    NCT = National City Transit   474-7505.
    NCTD= North County Transit District 722- or 743-6283.
    SDT = San Diego Transit   233-3004.
    Trolley = San Diego Trolley   231-8549.
    Routes 901, 932, 933, 934   232-8505
Information from: Telephone number for transit information.
Typical business hours: Usually the open hours for major
    retailers. The "+/-" indicates that some services are
    available earlier or later than hours listed.
Security patrol: Parking lot security patrols are noted here.
Public Rest Rooms: If available, how found.
Benches: Public rest seating is noted if available.
Restaurants: The type and amount of food services are listed.
Walks and distances: The first listing is usually walking on the
    mall store-front sidewalks or shopping center property.
Area walks range from short (4/10th mile) to long (2-2/10th
    miles) routes in areas adjoining the walking site.
    Wherever possible these walks are guided to face oncom-
    ing traffic. Only a few are in rural areas where
    sidewalks are lacking or in a reverse direction.
"Not feasible" indicates the walk is either very difficult or impos-
    sible due to construction or terrain.
"Not recommended" indicates an industrial or commercial area,
    or related problem, where walking may be hazardous.

Malls

Carlsbad

Plaza Camino Real

Description: A fully enclosed, air-conditioned, shopping mall
  with two levels both of which are suitable for mall walk-
  ing. It includes numerous major department stores. A
  small shopping center adjoins on the West.
Located at 2525 El Camino Real, Carlsbad, 92008.
Community/Area name: Carlsbad.
Thomas Guide: Map page 14, Grid A-2.
Intersection of Freeway 78, El Camino Real and Marron Road.
Parking entry from El Camino Real, Marron Road, Haymar
  Drive or Monroe Street.
Transit service via NCTD #302, #309, #312, #316, #320, #321,
  #322.   Schedule information from 722- or 743-6283.
  Also CTS #800. Schedule information from 233-3004.
The Plaza is a major transit center with numerous lines ter-
  minating at a station in the south parking lot.
Typical business hours: 0900 to2100 +/-.
Air-conditioning: The mall is fully air-conditioned.
Security patrol: Yes. Both mall and parking lot have security
  patrols during all hours.
Public Rest Rooms: Mapped on Directory Board.   Benches: Yes.
Restaurants: An extensive selection of snacks and fast foods are
  available. Dining houses are in an adjoining area.
Mall walking program sponsored by Mission Park Medical
Clinic. Information from 967-4985.
                Mall Walking in San Diego County

Plaza Camino Real   **Carlsbad**

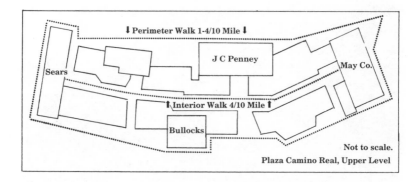

Walks and distances: The upper and lower levels are 4/10th (.4)
    mile long. A walk around the perimeter of the central
    building will total 1-4/10th (1.4) miles.
An easy area walk of 2-8/10 (2.8) miles begins on El Camino
    Real. Walk right (South) to Marron Road and turn right.
    Walk West to the far end of Marron Road and the
    entrance to North County Plaza. Go right (East) through
    North County Plaza to Monroe Street, then left (North)
    through that portion of the large parking lot nearest
    Freeway 78. Continue to El Camino Real and beginning.

Mall Walking in San Diego County

El Cajon

Parkway Plaza Shopping Center

Description: A recently expanded and refurbished mall with
large department stores and an extensive variety of
boutique and community service retailers.

Located at 415 Fletcher Parkway.

City El Cajon, 92020.

Community/Area name: El Cajon.

Thomas Guide: Map page 56, Grid B-3.

Intersection of Interstate 8 and Freeway 67.

Parking entry from Fletcher Parkway or Pioneer Street. The lat-
ter has a traffic signal to assist in exiting..

Transit service via SDT #115. CTS #846, 847, 848, 858, 864,
881-885, 888 and 894.

Schedule information from 233-3004.

Typical business hours: 1000 to 2100 +/-.

Air-conditioning. The central complex is air conditioned.

Security Patrol: Yes.   Public Rest Rooms on Directory Board.

Benches: There are many benches on which to rest.

Restaurants: The Food Court offers a wide variety of services.

Mall walking program sponsored by Parkway Plaza.
Information from 579-7795.

Parkway Plaza Shopping Center   # El Cajon

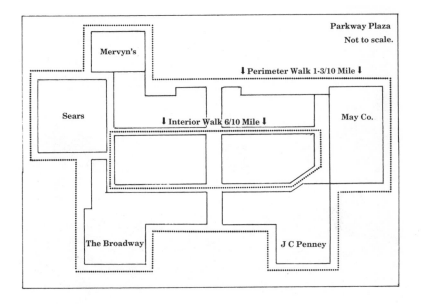

Walks and distances: The inside square walkway of the mall is
6/10th (.6) of a mile in length.
A perimeter walk of the central complex will total 1-1/3rd (1.3)
miles. When construction of the Broadway Department
store is completed, add 1/10th (.1) mile.
Due to heavy traffic, and industrial/commercial activity surrounding the mall, area walks are not recommended.

Mall Walking in San Diego County

El Centro, Imperial County

Description: A medium-size shopping mall, recently refurbished,
with adjoining strip stores and community services.
Located at 1601 Main Street, El Centro, 92243.
Community/Area name: El Centro.
Thomas Guide: Map page 410, Grid C-3. Imperial County.
Transit service via Goodalls' Imperial County Transit. All four
motor coaches stop at the Valley Plaza.
Schedule Information from 353-3520.
Typical business hours: 0900 to 2200 +/-.
Air-conditioning: The central complex is air conditioned.
Security Patrol: Yes   Public Rest Rooms: No.
Benches: There are many benches on which to rest.
Restaurants: Snack services are available.

Mall Walking in San Diego County

Valley Plaza   # El Centro, Imperial County

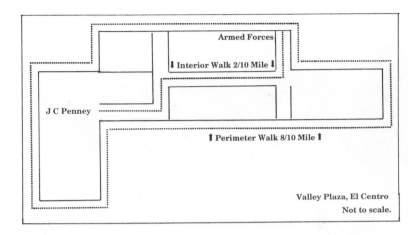

Armed Forces

↓ Interior Walk 2/10 Mile ↓

J C Penney

↑ Perimeter Walk 8/10 Mile ↑

Valley Plaza, El Centro
Not to scale.

Walks and distances: The longest inside hallway of the mall is
2/10th (.2) of a mile in length from Armed Services
Recruiting to the J.C.Penney store.
A perimeter walk of the central complex is 8/10th (.8) of a mile.
An area walk of one mile (1.0) begins on Main Street. Walk left
to Waterman Avenue, go left to Brighton Avenue, left on
Imperial Avenue to Main, and turn left to the beginning.

Mall Walking in San Diego County

Escondido

Description: An older enclosed mall which is being converted to
a strip shopping center. Some mall walking may be pos-
sible when reconstruction is completed.
Located at 1261 East Valley Parkway, Escondido, 92025.
Community/Area name: Escondido.
Thomas Guide: Map page 22, Grid F-1.
Intersection of East Valley Parkway and Ash Street.
Parking entry from East Valley Parkway or Ash Street.
Transit service via NCTD # 381.
    Information from 722- or 743-6283.
Typical business hours: 0900 to 2100 +/-.
Air-conditioning: The mall portion of the structure was air-
conditioned. Stores in the strip section are individually
air-conditioned.
Security patrol. Unknown.
Public Rest Rooms. No.   Benches: Yes.
Restaurants: Dining in the area and snack foods in Mall.

Mall Walking in San Diego County

Escondido Village Mall　　　　　　　　　**Escondido**

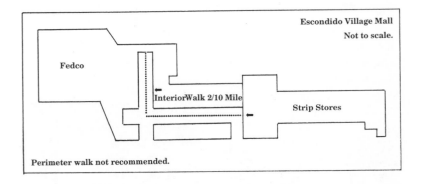

Walks and distances: The enclosed hallway of the mall is 2/10th
(.2) of a mile long.
A 2-1/2 (2.5) mile area walk begins on East Valley Parkway.
Walk left (West) to Ash Street and turn left. Continue on
Ash (South) to Grand Avenue and turn left. Follow
Grand (East) to Rose, go left (North) to East Valley
Parkway, then left (West) to the point of beginning.

No formal mall walking program at the present time.

Mall Walking in San Diego County

Escondido North County Fair

Description: A major upscale enclosed shopping mall on two and
three levels. Wide variety of food services ranging from
snacks to fine dining. A small park is behind the mall.
Located at 200 East Via Rancho Parkway, Escondido, 92026.
Community/Area name: Escondido.
Thomas Guide: Map page 27, Grid F-2.
Intersection of Interstate 15 and Via Rancho Parkway.
Parking entry from Via Rancho Parkway or Beethoven Drive.
Transit service via SDT #20.   Information from 233-3004.
          Also NCTD #382, #384.   Information 722- or 743-6283.
          There is a transit station behind North County Fair on
          Beethoven Street.
Typical business hours: 1000 to 2100 +/-.
Air-conditioning: All levels of the mall are fully air-conditioned.
Security patrol: Yes. Both parking lot and interior areas have
          security patrols
Public Rest Rooms: Mapped on the directory board. They are on
          the third level with food services.
Benches: There are numerous places to rest including the park
          area behind North County Fair.
Restaurants: An extensive selection of food services are avail-
          able inside and outside the mall.
Mall walking program sponsored by North County Fair.
Information from 489-2332.
Mall Walking in San Diego County

North County Fair   **Escondido**

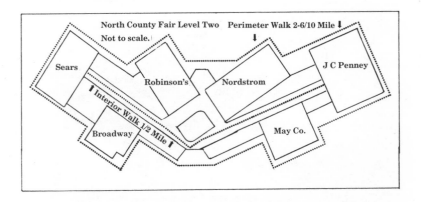

North County Fair Level Two   Perimeter Walk 2-6/10 Mile

Not to scale.

Sears

Robinson's   Nordstrom

J C Penney

Interior Walk 1/2 Mile

Broadway

May Co.

Walks and distances: There are three walks available inside the
   mall. The first level is 3/10th (.3) of a mile from J.C. Penney to the Rotunda. The second level is 1/2 (.5) mile from
   J.C. Penney to Sears. The third level is 1/4 (.25) mile
   from Sears to Nordstroms.
A pleasant walk of 2-6/10th (2.6) miles is around the building's
   perimeter. This includes a small park area on the North
   side and a variety of sidewalk wanderings.
An area walk, of 3-4/10th (3.4) miles begins on Beethoven Street.
   Exit the mall on a passageway between Nordstroms and
   Robinsons department stores. Beethoven street is
   directly ahead. Turn left up the slight rise for a bridge
   over Interstate 15 which curves down toward Via
   Rancho Parkway. At Via Rancho turn left, bridging the
   freeway again, and continue past North County Fair to
   the other end of Beethoven Street. Turn left (West) to
   the point of beginning. This is a nice workout.

Mall Walking in San Diego County

National City

Description: This is an impressive enclosed mall anchored by
    major department stores and an excellent selection of
    retail outlets with community services.
Located at 3030 East Plaza Bonita Road. National City, 92050.
Community/Area name: National City.
Thomas Guide: Map page 69, Grid E-2.
Intersection of Freeway 805 and South Bay Parkway (State 54).
Parking entry from Sweetwater Road, Ring Road or Plaza
    Bonita Road.
Transit service via NCT #601, #602, #604.Information 474-7505.
    Also: CVT # 705, #705A. Information from 476-9914.
Typical business hours: 1000 to 2100 +/-.
Air-conditioning. The entire complex is air conditioned.
Security Patrol: Yes.   Public Rest Rooms on Directory Board.
Benches: There are many benches on which to rest.
Restaurants: A wide variety of snack and fast food services are
    available inside the Plaza.
Mall walking program sponsored by Paradise Valley Hospital.
Information from 470-4281.

Mall Walking in San Diego County

Plaza Bonita

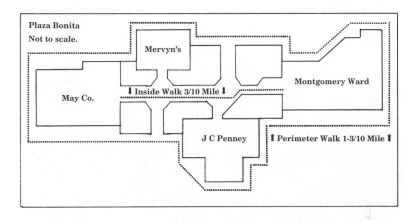

Walks and distances: The longest inside hallway in the mall is
3/10th (.3) of a mile in length.
A perimeter walk of the central structure will total 1-1/3rd (1.3)
miles. It is necessary to wander through parking lots,
use entry streets and one flight of stairs in walking
around the building.
Due to the Plaza's location, amid freeways and busy surface
streets, area walking is not recommended. However
there is a small County Park in the South-West corner of
the property which is suitable for outdoor strolling.

Mall Walking in San Diego County

San Diego

Description: The centerpiece of San Diego shopping centers
which, although not a mall, offers an interesting facility
for walking and stair climbing. There are two theatres.
Located at Fourth and Broadway, San Diego, 92101.
Community/Area name: San Diego Downtown.
Thomas Guide: Map page 65, Grid C-2.
Intersection of Broadway and Fourth Avenue.
Parking entry into multi-level garages from Fourth Avenue, "G"
Street or First Avenue.
Transit service: All Downtown bus routes pass Horton Plaza.
The main San Diego Trolley line is one block west.
Schedule information from 233-3004.
Typical business hours: 1000 to 2100 +/-.
Air-conditioning. Individual stores. The central walking area is
open to the sky.
Security Patrol: Yes, in both shopping and parking areas.
Public Rest Rooms are not shown on the Directory Board. One is
past the Jessops' clock, on the left of Level 1. The other
is on Level 2 adjacent to Abercrombie & Fitch.
Benches: There are many benches on which to rest.
Restaurants: The Food Court offers a wide variety of services.
Mall walking program sponsored by Oasis located in Robinson's
Department Store. Information from 531-1131.

Mall Walking in San Diego County

Horton Plaza   **San Diego**

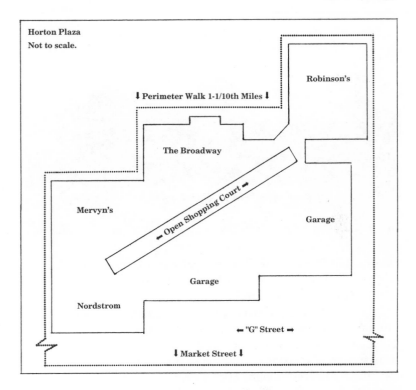

Horton Plaza
Not to scale.

↓ Perimeter Walk 1-1/10th Miles ↓

Robinson's

The Broadway

← Open Shopping Court →

Mervyn's

Garage

Garage

Nordstrom

← "G" Street →

↓ Market Street ↓

Walks and distances: The inside of Horton Plaza is best for stair
    climbing, and there are many, or strolling. Elevators and
    escalators serve all floors.
A walk around the Plaza is 1-1/10th (1.1) miles. Exit the Plaza
    onto Broadway and turn left. At First Avenue go left to
    Market Street and turn left into San Diego's famous
    Gaslamp Quarter. Continue ahead to Fourth Avenue, go
    left to Broadway and left again to the point of beginning.

Mall Walking in San Diego County

San Diego

Description: This is a well-known tourist attraction which, by
virtue of its waterfront location, offers unusual opportunities for walking.

Located at 849 West Harbor Drive, San Diego, 92101.

Community/Area name: San Diego, Downtown.

Thomas Guide: Map page 65, Grid B-2.

Intersection of Harbor Drive and Pacific Highway.

Parking entry from Pacific Highway.

Transit service via SDT #7, #7B.　　　Information from 233-3004.

Typical business hours: 0900 to 2200 +/-.

Air-conditioning. Individual buildings.

Security Patrol: Yes.

Public Rest Rooms are mapped on the Directory Board.

Benches: There are many benches on which to rest.

Restaurants: The Village offers a wide variety of menus and
theme houses, including over-water dining.

Mall Walking in San Diego County

Seaport Village   # San Diego

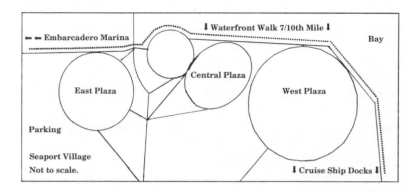

Seaport Village
Not to scale.

Walks and distances: A moderate waterfront walk of 7/10th (.7) of a mile begins at the Marriott hotel on the South-East and leads along the waterfront to Harbor Drive. It is possible to walk further to cruise ship docks and a maritime museum further North. The Embarcadero Marina Park is on the far side of the Marriott Hotel.

No formal mall walking program at the present time.

Mall Walking in San Diego County

Shopping Centers

Alpine

Description: A small rustic theme center providing shopping
　　services for this rural community.
Located at 1347 Tavern Road, Alpine, 92001.
Community/Area name: Alpine.
Thomas Guide: Page 50, Grid F-5.
Intersection of Tavern Road and Alpine Boulevard.
Transit service via CTS # 864.　　　　Information from 233-3004.
Typical business hours: 0700 to 2100 +/-.
Security Patrol: Yes, evenings.
Public Rest Rooms: No.　　　　　　　　　　　Benches: No.
Restaurants: Food service is available in the center.
Walks and distances: A walk around the central building com-
　　plex will total 4/10 (.4) of a mile.
An area walk begins by exiting onto Tavern Road. Go left
　　(uphill) to Arnold, turn left and continue about one-half
　　mile to Alpine Boulevard. Make a sharp reverse left and
　　walk down Alpine to Tavern, go left uphill to the point of
　　beginning. This is 1-4/10 (1.4) miles.

Mall Walking in San Diego County

River Village   **Bonsall**

Description: A new community center which is planned for a mix
    of specialty shopping opportunities, indoor and outdoor
    food services, and a six-screen theatre.
Located at 5256 South Mission Road, Bonsall, 92003.
Community/Area name: Bonsall.
Thomas Guide: Page 8, Grid E-1.
Intersection of Highway 76 and Mission Road.
Transit service via NCTD #306 to Fallbrook.
    Information from 722- or 743-6283.
Typical business hours: Not established at time of printing.
Security patrol: Yes.
Public Rest Rooms: Yes; in each of the major buildings.
    Benches: No.
Restaurants: Plans include extensive eating facilities.
Walks and distances: Best for center strolls. Perimeter and area
    walks not feasible due to incomplete public sidewalks
    and velocity of highway traffic.

Mall Walking in San Diego County

Borrego Springs   **The Mall**

Description: Despite its name, this is an open-air community
          service center containing banks, boutique shops and
          dining establishments.
Located at 547 Palm Canyon Drive, Borrego Springs, 92004.
Community/Area name: Borrego Springs.
Thomas Guide: Page 77, Grid B-6.
Intersection of Palm Canyon Drive and Country Club Road.
Transit service via CTS #882, #883. Information from 233-3004.
Typical business hours: 1000 to 1600 +/-.
Security patrol: Unknown.
Public Rest Rooms: Yes, in central hallway.   Benches: Yes.
Restaurants: Several, including a coffee shop which serves
          "Buffalo Burgers" made of ground buffalo meat.
Walks and distances: The longest open hallway is 2/10th (.2) of a
          mile in length, including several short flights of steps.
A walk around the perimeter will total 4/10th (.4) of a mile.
Area walking is only suitable during morning or late afternoon
          hours when the desert heat moderates. Summer tem-
          peratures are excessive for walking exercise.

Mall Walking in San Diego County

Carlsbad Plaza   **Carlsbad**

Description: Small strip shopping center with a chain food out-
      let, major drug store and other community services.
Located at 2650 El Camino Real, Carlsbad, 92008.
Community/Area name: Carlsbad.
Thomas Guide: Page 14, Grid B-2.
Intersection of El Camino Real and Haymar Drive.
Transit service via NCTD #332. A number of other lines ter-
      minate across the street at Plaza Camino Real.
      Information from 722- or 743-6283.
Typical business hours: 0600 to 2400 +/-.
Security patrol: Unknown.
Public Rest Rooms: No.   Benches: No.
Restaurants: Several dining houses are in the center.
Walks and distances: Best for strolling. See Plaza El Camino
      Real, in Carlsbad, for mall and perimeter walks.

Mall Walking in San Diego County

Carlsbad

Description: A small strip center south of Carlsbad Plaza.
Located at 2602 El Camino Real, Carlsbad, 92008.
Community/Area name: Carlsbad.
Thomas Guide: Page 14, Grid B-2.
Intersection of El Camino Real and Marron Road.
Transit service via NCTD #322.   Information 722- or 743-6283.
Typical business hours: 0900 to 1800 +/-.
Security patrol: Unknown.
Public Rest Rooms: No.   Benches: No.
Restaurants: Several sources of lunch or light snacks.
Walks and distances: Best for strolling. See Plaza El Camino
        Real, in Carlsbad, for mall and perimeter walks.

Mall Walking in San Diego County

Rancho San Diego Village   **Casa de Oro**

Description: A large diversified community shopping center also
known as the Spring Valley Shopping Center.
Located at 3681 Avocado Boulevard, Spring Valley, 92077
Community/Area name: Casa de Oro (La Mesa).
Thomas Guide: Page 63, Grid C-4.
Intersection of Avocado Boulevard and Freeway 94.
Transit service via SDT #856.   Information from 233-3004.
Typical business hours: 0600 to 2400 +/-.
Security patrol: Yes.
Public Rest Rooms: No.   Benches: No.
Restaurants: A wide selection from dining to snacks.
Walks and distances: The store-front sidewalks total 3/10th (.3)
of a mile for both major complexes.
Area walks are not feasible due to proximity of Freeway 94 and
restricted access residential developments.

Mall Walking in San Diego County

Chollas Creek

Metropolitan Center

Description: Small strip shopping center of community services.
Located at 1755 54th Street, San Diego, 92105.
Community/Area name: Chollas Creek.
Thomas Guide: Page 61, Grid D-6.
Intersection of 54th St. and Euclid Avenue at Westover Place.
Transit service via SDT #5, #105   Information from 233-3004.
Typical business hours: 0900 to 2100 +/-.
Security patrol: Unknown.
Public Rest Rooms: No.   Benches: No.
Restaurants: Snack service is available.
Walks and distances: Not feasible for walking due to construc-
        tion and area traffic.

Mall Walking in San Diego County

Chula Vista Center   **Chula Vista**

Description: A large upscale community shopping center with a
        pleasant (4/10th mile) open "mall".
Located at 555 Broadway, Chula Vista, 92010.
Community/Area name: Chula Vista.
Thomas Guide: Page 69, Grid D-5.
Intersection of Broadway and "H" Street.
Transit service via CVT #703 or #706.   Information 233-3004
Typical business hours: 0900 to 2100 +/-
Security patrol: Yes.
Public Rest Rooms: Yes.   Benches: Yes.
Restaurants: Wide variety of specialty eating houses.
Walks and distances: The Center's open mall is 4/10th (.4) of a
        mile in length. A perimeter walk of the Center buildings
        will total 1-6/10th (1.6) miles.
A two mile (2.0) area walk begins on "H" Street. Walk left (West)
        to Broadway and turn left. Continue South to "I" Street
        and go left again. Remain on "I" to Fig Avenue and turn
        left, then ahead to "H" Street where you turn left and
        continue ahead to the point of beginning.

Mall Walking in San Diego County

Clairemont

Description: A medium-size shopping center with major food,
     drug and clothing chain outlets.
Located at 5555 Balboa Avenue, San Diego, 92117.
Community/Area name: Clairemont.
Thomas Guide: Page 53, Grid B-2.
Intersection of Balboa Avenue and Genesee Avenue.
Transit service via SDT #27, #41.   Information from 233-3004.
Typical business hours: 0600 to 2400 +/-.
Security patrol: Unknown.
Public Rest Rooms: No.   Benches: No.
Restaurants: Food service is available in the center.
Walks and distances: It is 4/10th (.4) of a mile around buildings
     of the largest complex. The smaller section is not
     suitable for perimeter walking.
A one-mile area walk begins on Balboa Avenue. Go left (West) to
     Genesee Avenue and turn left (South) to Mount Alifan
     Drive. Walk left on Mount Alifan to Balboa Avenue and
     continue left (West) to the point of beginning.

Mall Walking in San Diego County

Clairemont Square   **Clairemont**

Description: A large shopping center with theatres, food outlets,
   restaurants and snack services. Adjoining is Clairemont
   Village Shopping Center under the same management.
Located at 3900 Clairemont Mesa Boulevard, San Diego, 92117.
Community/Area name: Clairemont.
Thomas Guide: Page 44, Grid E-6.
Intersection of Clairemont Mesa Blvd. and Clairemont Drive.
Transit service via SDT #4, #5, #25, #50, #105, #150.
Information from 233-3004.
Typical business hours: 0600 to 2400 +/-.
Security patrol: Yes.
Public Rest Rooms: Yes; near the south-east entrance.
Benches: Yes.
Restaurants: There are several restaurants and snack services.
Walks and distances: A perimeter walk around the main build-
   ing will total 9/10th (.9) of a mile.
An area walk of 1-2/10th (1.2) miles begins by exiting the shop-
   ping center onto Clairemont Mesa Boulevard. Walk left
   (East) to Clairemont Drive, go North-West on
   Clairemont Drive until it rejoins Clairemont Mesa
   Boulevard. Turn left and continue to the beginning. All
   of these streets curve left to complete a loop.

Mall Walking in San Diego County

Clairemont

Description: Medium-size full-service shopping center.
Located at 3001 Clairemont Drive, San Diego, 92117.
Community/Area name: Clairemont.
Thomas Guide: Page 52, Grid F-4.
Intersection of Clairemont Drive and Burgener.
Transit service via SDT #5.   Information from 233-3004.
Typical business hours: 0700 to 2100 +/-.
Security patrol: Unknown.
Public Rest Rooms: No.   Benches: No.
Restaurants: Sit-down dining, fast food and snacks available.
Walks and distances: The store-front sidewalk is 2/10th (.2) of a
    mile long.
A one-mile area walk begins on Clairemont Drive. Walk left
    (South-West) to Burgener, turn left and go (South-East)
    to Field Street. Go left (North-East) to Cowley Way and
    continue on Cowley to Iroquois Avenue. Turn left (West)
    and continue to Clairemont Drive, then left to point of
    beginning.
Walking paths of Tecolote Canyon Natural Park are at the East
    end of Iroquois Avenue.

Mall Walking in San Diego County

Convoy Plaza   **Clairemont**

Description: A medium-size shopping center with major retail
            chain stores and a service station.
Located at 4220 Balboa Avenue, San Diego, 92117.
Community/Area name: Clairemont.
Thomas Guide: Page 53, Grid D-1.
Intersection of Balboa Avenue and Convoy Street.
Transit service via SDT #27.   Information from 233-3004.
Typical business hours: 0600 to 2400 +/-.
Security patrol: Unknown.
Public Rest Rooms: No.   Benches: No.
Restaurants: Located at the west end of the center.
Walks and distances: It is not possible to walk around the
            central building perimeter.
An area walk of 6/10th (.6) mile is possible. Go to the West end
            of the parking lot, nearest Freeway 805, turn left (South)
            and exit onto Armour Street. Go left (East) on Armour to
            Ruffner Street, turn left (North) to Balboa Avenue and
            turn left again. Continue on Balboa to the western entry
            into the parking lot, enter and continue South to the
            point of beginning in the parking lot.

Mall Walking in San Diego County

Clairemont

Description: A large multi-service shopping center.
Located at 4283 Genesee Street, San Diego, 92117.
Community/Area name: Clairemont.
Thomas Guide: Page 53, Grid A-1.
Intersection of Balboa Avenue and Genesee Street.
Transit service via SDT #27, #41.   Information from 233-3004.
Typical business hours: 0600 to 2400 +/-.
Security patrol: Unknown.
Public Rest Rooms: No.   Benches: No.
Restaurants: A wide variety of menus and prices are available.
Walks and distances: A store-front walk, from 4Day Tire to the
    Home Depot, will total 4/10th (.4) of a mile.
A walk around the buildings is 7/10th (.7) of a mile.
A 1-2/10th (1.2) mile walk in the surrounding residential area
    begins by exiting onto Balboa Avenue. Walk left (East) to
    Mount Abernathy Avenue, turn left (North-West) to
    reach Balboa Arms Drive and left again to Derrick
    Drive. Go left (South) to Genesee Avenue, turn left onto
    Balboa and continue to the point of beginning.

Mall Walking in San Diego County

Coronado Plaza   **Coronado**

Description: A small triangular professional center with retail
      shops, food services and underground parking.
Located at 1330 Orange Avenue, Coronado, 92118.
Community/Area name: Coronado.
Thomas Guide: Page 65, Grid B-5.
Intersection of Orange Avenue with Churchill Place and Dana
      Place.
Transit service via MTS #901.   Information from 233-3004.
Typical business hours: 0900 to 1800 +/-.
Security patrol: Underground garage attendant.
Public Rest Rooms: Yes.   Benches: No.
Restaurants: Dining facilities are available.
Walks and distances: It is 3/10th (.3) of a mile around the Plaza.
One block to the South-West is the Municipal Beach with exten-
      sive walking paths and access to the sand. A nearby
      lifeguard facility can provide information.

Mall Walking in San Diego County

Coronado Old Ferry Landing

Description: Small nautical theme center with boutique and
        souvenir shops, and the San Diego Ferry landing dock.
Located at 1201 First Street, Coronado, 92118.
Community/Area name: Coronado.
Thomas Guide: Page 65, Grid B-3.
Intersection of First Street and "B" Avenue.
Transit service via SDT #19. MTS #901.
        Information from 233-3004.
Typical business hours: 0900 to 2100 +/-.
Security patrol: Yes.
Public Rest Rooms: Yes. Inquire at Office #120.   Benches: Yes.
Restaurants: Fast food service and snacks are available.
Walks and distances: The theme center is suitable for strolling.
A waterfront paved walkway leads South-East to the Tidelands
        Park which is about one mile to the right. Walking to the
        left on the waterfront pathway provides excellent views
        of the bay and buildings of downtown San Diego.

Mall Walking in San Diego County

Del Mar Heights   **Del Mar**

Description: A small community services shopping center.
Located at 2600 Del Mar Heights Road, Del Mar, 92014.
Community/Area name: Del Mar.
Thomas Guide: Page 34, Grid B-4.
Intersection of Del Mar Heights Road and Mango Drive.
Parking entry from Del Mar Heights Road or Mango Drive.
Transit service not available.
Typical business hours: 0700 to 2400 +/-.
Security patrol: Unknown.
Public Rest Rooms: No.   Benches: No.
Restaurants: A limited selection including snack food.
Walks and distances: The sidewalk fronting all stores is 2/10 (.2)
    mile long. A walk around the complex is 1/2 (.5) mile.
A 1-2/10 (1.2) mile area walk begins by exiting west onto Mango
    Drive. Go left (South) to Del Mar Heights Road and turn
    to the right (West) uphill to Boquita Drive. Go right
    (North) to Vantage Way and turn right again. Follow
    Vantage east to Mango Drive. Turn right (South) on
    Mango to point of beginning. There is some up/down
    walking while following this residential route.

Mall Walking in San Diego County

Del Mar

Description: A small multi-level shopping center with an under-
ground garage, boutique stores and a wide selection of
ocean-view restaurants for fine dining.
Located at 1555 Camino del Mar, Del Mar, 92014.
Community/Area name: Del Mar.
Thomas Guide: Page 34, Grid A-2.
Intersection of Camino del Mar and 15th Street.
Parking entry into garage from Camino del Mar or 15th Street.
Transit service via NCTD #301, #308.
    Information from 722- or 743-6283.
Typical business hours: 0900 to 1900 +/-.
Air-conditioning: Individual stores and ocean breeze.
Security patrol: Unknown.
Public Rest Rooms: No.   Elevator: Yes.   Benches: Yes.
Restaurants: A good selection, most with an ocean view.
Walks and distances: There are many stairways for strolling the
complex. Building perimeter walking is not possible.
A charming uphill/downhill walk of 1-1/2 (1.5) miles is possible.
    Exit West onto Camino del Mar, turn left (South) and
    walk to 15th Street. Left (East) uphill to Luneta Drive,
    go left (North) to Primavera, right (East) a few feet to
    Serpentine on the left. Follow Serpentine (North) to Bel-
    laire Street, turn left (West) on Bellaire to Sea Vista
    Avenue. Go left (West) downhill to Camino del Mar, then
    left (South) to beginning. There are few sidewalks.

Mall Walking in San Diego County

Fletcher Hills Town & Country   # El Cajon

Description: A large community services shopping center.
Located at 2810 Fletcher Hills Parkway, El Cajon, 92020.
Community/Area name: Fletcher Hills.
Thomas Guide: Page 55, Grid E-3.
Intersection of Navajo Road and Fletcher Parkway.
Transit service via SDT #115. CTS #858.
　　　Information from 233-3004.
Typical business hours: 0600 to 2400 +/-.
Security patrol: Unknown.
Public Rest Rooms: No.   Benches: No.
Restaurants: A wide variety of snack and fast food services plus
　　　seated dining in adjacent restaurants.
Walks and distances: The store-front sidewalk is 3/10th (.3) of a
　　　mile long. The building perimeter is 6/10th (.6) mile.
An interesting one-mile area walk begins at the South-East cor-
　　　ner into a park-like street marked "T & C Apartments".
　　　Continue ahead to Chatham Street, go right to Garden
　　　Grove on the left. Follow Garden Grove South (It be-
　　　comes Tahoe Street.) to Holly Oak Drive. Walk right
　　　(North) to Chatham, turn right (East) to the tree-shaded
　　　lane and proceed uphill to the beginning.

Mall Walking in San Diego County

El Cajon

Description: A group of small shopping centers including
    Johnson Center, Parkway Center and Broadway Plaza.
    Home furnishings and auto services predominate.
Located at 790 Johnson Avenue, El Cajon, 92020.
Community/Area name: El Cajon.
Thomas Guide: Page 56, Grid B-3 and C-3.
Intersections of Fletcher Parkway, Johnson Avenue, Arnele
    Avenue and Jackman Street.
Transit service via SDT #115. CTS #846, #847, #848, #858,
    #864, #881-885, #888, #894. Information from 233-3004.
Typical business hours: 0900 to 2100 +/-.
Security patrol: Unknown.
Public Rest Rooms: No.   Benches: No.
Restaurants: Both dining and fast-food services are available.
Walks and distances: Continual vehicle activity within the cen-
    ters, and heavy traffic on surrounding streets, suggest
    that walking is not feasible.

Mall Walking in San Diego County

Plaza de Las Palmas   **El Cajon**

Description: Recently opened small community shopping center.
Located at 1201 Avocado Boulevard, El Cajon, 92020.
Community/Area name: El Cajon.
Thomas Guide: Page 56, Grid C-6.
Intersection of Avocado Boulevard and Chase Avenue.
Transit service via CTS #852.   Information from 233-3004.
Typical business hours: 0600 to 2400 +/-.
Security patrol: Unknown.
Public Rest Rooms: No.   Benches: No.
Restaurants: Snacks and fast food are available.
Walks and distances: The store-front sidewalk is 2/10th (.2) of a
    mile long. It is 1/2 (.5) mile around the perimeter of the
    main building.
A residential area walk of 7/10th (.7) mile begins by exiting onto
    Chase Avenue. Turn right and walk to Burnaby Street.
    Go up Burnaby (South) to Coldstream Drive on the left.
    Follow Coldstream to Mollison Avenue, go left (North) to
    Chase, turn left and continue to the point of beginning.

Mall Walking in San Diego County

Encinitas

Description: A medium-size community shopping center.
Located at 131 North El Camino Real, Encinitas, 92024.
Community/Area name: Encinitas.
Thomas Guide: Page 25, Grid B-4.
Intersection of El Camino Real and Via Molina.
Transit service via NCTD #304, #309, #391.
          Information from 722- or 743-6283.
Typical business hours: 0900 to 2100 +/-.
Security patrol: Unknown.
Public Rest Rooms: No.   Benches: No.
Restaurants: Several eateries are available in the center.
Walks and distances: Walking the sidewalks of all three retail
          buildings will total 4/10th (.4) of a mile.
A walk around the perimeter of the three buildings totals 6/10th
          (.6) of a mile.
A fine 2-6/10th (2.6) mile area walk begins on El Camino Real.
          Walk left to Encinitas Boulevard and turn left (East)
          uphill. Go to Village Park Way, turn left (North) and
          continue on Village Park to Mountain Vista Drive. Go
          left, downhill, to El Camino Real and walk left to the
          point of beginning. This is a pleasant residential area of-
          fering a modest amount of uphill/downhill walking.

Mall Walking in San Diego County

Wiegand Plaza   **Encinitas**

Description: A quality shopping center, with a theatre, spread
        over two blocks. Camino Village Plaza is in a third block
        adjoining Wiegand Plaza on the north.
Located at 100 and 200 North El Camino Real, Encinitas, 92024.
Community/Area name: Encinitas.
Thomas Guide: Page 25, Grid A-4.
Intersection of El Camino Real and Via Molina.
Parking entry from Via Molina or El Camino Real.
Transit service via NCTD #304, #309, #361.
        Information from 722- or 743-6283.
Typical business hours: 0600 to 2200 +/-.
Security patrol: Unknown.
Public Rest Rooms: No.   Benches: No.
Restaurants: A wide variety of both dining and fast foods.
Walks and distances: It is 3/10th (.3) mile along store-front
        sidewalks of the two complexes.
There is a long 1-8/10th (1.8) mile walk possible through a good
        residential area. Exit onto El Camino Real and walk left
        (north) to Via Montoro. Turn left (West) and go uphill to
        Via Cantebria. Go left (downhill and South) on Via Can-
        tebria to Encinitas Boulevard, turn left and continue
        East to El Camino Real. Go left (North) to beginning.

Mall Walking in San Diego County

Escondido
Del Norte Plaza

Description: A medium-size community shopping center with a
theatre and fine selection of restaurants.
Located at 350 West El Norte Parkway, Escondido, 92025.
Community/Area name: Escondido.
Thomas Guide: Page 17, Grid C-5.
Intersection of Centre City Parkway and El Norte Parkway.
Transit service via NCTD #385.
Information from 722- or 743-6283.
Typical business hours: 0600 to 2300 +/-.
Security patrol: Yes.
Public Rest Rooms: No. Benches: No.
Restaurants: There are several excellent dining establishments.
Walks and distances: The center is best for strolling. A property
perimeter walk is not feasible. On the other side of El
Norte Parkway is a residential complex which offers op-
portunities for long and short walking ventures.

Mall Walking in San Diego County

Escondido Promenade   **Escondido**

Description: A long medium-size shopping center with many
    major stores and community services.
Located at 1280 Auto Park Way, Escondido, 92025.
Community/Area name: Escondido.
Thomas Guide: Page 22, Grid C-3.
Intersection of Auto Park Way, Valley Parkway and 9th Avenue.
Transit service via NCTD #382.
        Information from 722- or 743-6283.
Typical business hours: 0900 to 2100 +/-.
Security patrol: Unknown.
Public Rest Rooms: No.   Benches: No.
Restaurants: A wide variety of food services are available.
Walks and distances: The store-front sidewalk is 6/10th (.6) mile
    from 9th Street to Valley Parkway.
A 1-3/10th (1.3) mile walk begins on Auto Park Way. Walk left
    (South) to the 9th Street Promenade entrance, continue
    left (North) on the store-front sidewalk to Valley
    Parkway and go left (South) to the point of beginning.

Mall Walking in San Diego County

Escondido

Description:A small community service center with food chain
and drug store anchors.
Located at 640 North Escondido Boulevard, Escondido, 92025.
Community/Area name: Escondido.
Thomas Guide: Page 22, Grid D-2.
Intersection of North Escondido Boulevard and Washington Ave.
Transit service via NCTD #384, #385.
Information from 722- or 743-6283.
Typical business hours: 0800 to 2200 +/-.
Security patrol: Unknown.
Public Rest Rooms:No.   Benches: No.
Restaurants: Snacks and fast-food available.
Walks and distances: Best for strolling.

Mall Walking in San Diego County

Felicita Village   **Escondido**

Description: A small community shopping center with household
          services. On the other side of Felecita Avenue is Felecita
          Plaza with a major food store and additional facilities.
Located at 300 West Felecita, Escondido, 92025.
Community/Area name: Escondido.
Thomas Guide: Page 22, Grid E-4.
Intersection of Felecita Avenue and Escondido Boulevard.
Transit service via NCTD #381, #384.
          Information from 722- or 743-6283.
Typical business hours: 0900 to 2100 +/-.
Security patrol: Unknown.
Public Rest Rooms: No.   Benches: No.
Restaurants: Several lunch and snack facilities are available.
Walks and distances: Both the Village and Plaza are suitable for
          strolling. Area and perimeter walks are not feasible be-
          cause of the adjoining Centre City Parkway.

Mall Walking in San Diego County

Escondido

Description: A medium size strip center of limited services that
was formerly known as Midtown Plaza.
Located at 311 North Escondido Boulevard, Escondido, 92025.
Community/Area name: Escondido.
Thomas Guide: Page 22, Grid D-2.
Intersection of South Valley Parkway and N. Escondido Blvd.
Transit service via NCTD #384, #388.
Information from 722- or 743-6283.
Also via CTS #810. Information from 233-3004.
Typical business hours: 0900 to 1900 +/-.
Security patrol: Unknown.
Public Rest Rooms: No.   Benches: No.
Restaurants: Food services are available in the center.
Walks and distances: The store-front sidewalk is 2/10th (.2) mile
long. A building perimeter walk is not feasible. This
downtown location limits area walks to sidewalk strolls.

Mall Walking in San Diego County

The Vineyard   **Escondido**

Description: A unique three-level theme center with a theatre.
    Useful as a basing point for area walking.
Located at 1523 East Valley Parkway, Escondido, 92025.
Community/Area name: Escondido.
Thomas Guide: Page 23, Grid A-1.
Intersection of East Valley Parkway and Rose Street.
Transit service via NCTD #381.   Information 722- or 743-6283.
Typical business hours: 0900 to 1800 +/-.
Security patrol: Yes.
Public Rest Rooms: Yes.   Benches: Yes.
Restaurants: Several, offering excellent food.
Walks and distances: Excellent for strolling or stair climbing.
A 2-1/2 (2.5) mile area walk begins on East Valley Parkway.
    Walk left (West) to Ash Street and turn left. Continue
    South on Ash to Grand Avenue and turn left. Follow
    Grand (East) to Rose, go left (North) to East Valley
    Parkway, then left (West) to point of beginning.

Mall Walking in San Diego County

Fallbrook

Description: A small community shopping center.
Located at 1331 South Mission Road, Fallbrook, 92028.
Community/Area name: Fallbrook.
Thomas Guide: Page 5, Grid B-4.
Intersection of South Mission Road and Clemmens Lane.
Transit service via NCTD #306.   Information 722- or 743-6283.
Typical business hours: 0700 to 2300 +/-.
Security patrol: Unknown.
Public Rest Rooms: No.   Benches: No.
Restaurants: Snack food and lunches available.
Walks and distances: Strolling recommended. Area walking not
        feasible due to commercial/industrial activity.

Mall Walking in San Diego County

Fallbrook Towne Centre   **Fallbrook**

Description: Medium-size community shopping center offering a
        wide variety of services and materials.
Located at 1139 Mission Road, Fallbrook, 92028.
Community/Area name: Fallbrook.
Thomas Guide: Page 5, Grid C-5.
Intersection of Mission Road and Ammunition Road.
Transit service via NCTD #306.   Information 722- or 743-6283.
Typical business hours: 0600 to 2400 +/-.
Security patrol: Unknown.
Public Rest Rooms: No.   Benches: No.
Restaurants: There is a variety of dining and fast food outlets.
Walks and distances: Across Ammunition Road is a mid-range
        residential development which offers many opportunities
        for walks of any desired length. Light traffic makes
        walking the center's perimeter an easy venture.

Mall Walking in San Diego County

Grantville

Allied Gardens Shopping Center

Description: A medium-size strip shopping center with a food
      chain outlet, drug store and community service retailers.
Located at 5101 Waring Road, San Diego, 92120.
Community/Area name: Grantville.
Thomas Guide: Page 54, Grid D-5.
Intersection of Waring Road and Orcutt Avenue.
Transit service via SDT #13.   Information from 233-3004.
Typical business hours: 0600 to 2400 +/-.
Security patrol: Unknown.
Public Rest Rooms: No.   Benches: No.
Restaurants: Snacks and fast food are available.
Walks and distances: It is 3/10th (.3) of a mile around the
      perimeter of the center's main structure.
An area walk of 7/10th (.7) mile could begin on Waring Road.
         Walk to the left (South-West) to Orcutt Avenue and turn
         left. Continue (South-East) to Carthage Street. Walk left
         a few yards to Eldridge Street which is on the right, turn
         right and follow Eldridge to Zion Avenue. Go left
         (North-West) to Waring Road and point of beginning.
         This is a comfortable neighborhood walk.

Mall Walking in San Diego County

Friars Village   **Grantville**

Description: Three small shopping centers in a row at the point
         where Friars Road changes to Mission Gorge Road.
Located at 10330 Friars Road, San Diego, 92120.
Community/Area name: Grantville.
Thomas Guide: Page 54, Grid C-4.
Intersection of Friars Road and Mission Gorge Road.
Transit service via SDT #43.   Information from 233-3004.
Typical business hours: 0600 to 2200 +/-.
Security patrol: Unknown.
Public Rest Rooms: No.   Benches: No.
Restaurants: A wide selection of dining houses are in the three
         centers. Fast food and snack services are also available.
Walks and distances: Each of the three centers has a store-front
         sidewalk which is about 2/10th (.2) of a mile long.
A 4/10th (.4) mile area walk begins on Mission Gorge Road.
         Walk left (North) to Zion Avenue and turn left. Continue
         (West) on Zion to Riverdale Street, go left (South) to
         Friars Road and turn left (East) to the point of beginning
         where Friars changes to Mission Gorge. This is a short
         walk suitable for aggressive repetition.

Mall Walking in San Diego County

Kearny Mesa

Independence Square

Description: Small upscale service-oriented shopping center.
Located at 7305 Clairemont Mesa Boulevard, San Diego, 92111.
Community/Area name: Kearny Mesa.
Thomas Guide: Page 45, Grid C-6.
Intersection of Clairemont Mesa Boulevard and Ruffner Street.
Transit service via SDT #25.   Information from 233-3004.
Typical business hours: 0900 to 2100 +/-.
Security patrol: Unknown.
Public Rest Rooms: No.   Benches: No.
Restaurants: Both dining and snacks are available.
Walks and distances: The store-front sidewalk is 2/10th (.2) of a
     mile long.
Area walking is not feasible due to heavy traffic generated by
     surrounding industrial and commercial activity.

Mall Walking in San Diego County

Kearny Plaza   # Kearny Mesa

Description: This is a small strip of retail stores.
Located at 8199 Clairemont Mesa Boulevard, San Diego, 92117.
Community/Area name: Kearny Mesa.
Thomas Guide: Page 45, Grid D-6.
Intersection of Clairemont Mesa Boulevard and Mercury Street.
Transit service via SDT #25, #27.   Information from 233-3004.
Typical business hours: 0800 to 1800 +/-.
Security patrol: Unknown.
Public Rest Rooms: No.   Benches: No.
Restaurants: Fast foods and dining are available in the center.
Walks and distances: A perimeter walk around the central
    structure totals 3/10th (.3) of a mile.
Industrial and commercial activity in the area indicate that area
    walks are not recommended.

Mall Walking in San Diego County

Kearny Mesa

Description: A limited-service community center.
Located at 4688 Convoy Street, San Diego, 92111.
Community/Area name: Kearny Mesa.
Thomas Guide: Page 53, Grid C-1.
Intersection of Convoy Street and Engineer Road.
Transit service via SDT #27.　　　　Information from 233-3004.
Typical business hours: 0900 to 1800 +/-.
Security patrol: Unknown.
Public Rest Rooms: No.　　　　　　　　　　Benches: No.
Restaurants: Food service is available in the center.
Walks and distances: A walk around the building perimeter is
　　　3/10th (.3) of a mile.
A 7/10th (.7) mile area walk begins on Engineer Road. Turn left
　　　(West) and walk to Ruffner Street, go left (South) to Op-
　　　portunity Road and turn left again. Walk (East) to Con-
　　　voy Street, go left (North) to Engineer Road and left to
　　　the point of beginning. This is an industrial area with
　　　some shade trees and moderate traffic.

Mall Walking in San Diego County

Coast Walk **La Jolla**

Description: The most unique walking site in San Diego County
     although it is neither a shopping center or a mall.
Located at 1298 Prospect Street, San Diego, 92037.
Community/Area name: La Jolla.
Thomas Guide: Page 43-A, Grid F-1.
Intersection of Prospect Street and Ivanhoe Avenue.
Transit service via SDT #34.   Information from 233-3004.
Typical business hours: 1000 to 2200 +/-.
Security patrol: Unknown.
Public Rest Rooms: Yes, along the beach park pathways.
     Benches: Yes.
Restaurants: A variety of dining establishments with ocean
     views and extensive menus are in the building.
There is an elevator in the Coast Walk and multiple stairs to
     reach its numerous levels.
Walks and distances: It is only a short distance from Coast Walk
     to the La Jolla Beach area with its caves, Boomer Beach,
     Ellen Scripps Park, Alligator Head, La Jolla Cove and
     other interesting areas. There is a paved path along
     Scripps park above the beach. Stairs provide access to
     the waterfront for walks in sand and shallow water.

Mall Walking in San Diego County

La Jolla

Description: A large full-service community shopping center
  with upscale boutique stores and a theatre.
Located at 8657 Villa La Jolla Drive, San Diego, 92037.
Community/Area name: La Jolla.
Thomas Guide: Page 44, Grid C-2.
Intersection of Villa La Jolla Drive and Via Mallorca.
Transit service via SDT #34A, #50, #150.
  Information from 233-3004.
Typical business hours: 0800 to 2200 +/-.
Security patrol: Yes.
Public Rest Rooms: Yes, on the First Level near the east
  entrance. Inquire for directions.   Benches: Yes.
Restaurants: A wide variety of fast-food and dining estab-
  lishments are spread throughout the center.
Walks and distances: It is 7/10th (.7) of a mile around the
  central building.
A 1-1/2 (1.5) mile area walk begins on Villa La Jolla Drive. Walk
  left downhill (South) to Gilman Drive. Turn right, up
  Gilman (North), and continue to La Jolla Village Drive.
  Go right (East) on Village Drive to Villa La Jolla Drive,
  then turn right uphill (South) and continue to point of
  beginning in La Jolla Village Square.

Mall Walking in San Diego County

Baltimore West Shopping Center   **La Mesa**

Description: A small strip of retail stores.
Located at 5405 Baltimore Drive, La Mesa, 92041.
Community/Area name: La Mesa.
Thomas Guide: Page 55, Grid C-6.
Intersection of Baltimore Drive and Parkway Drive adjacent to
      I-8 Freeway.
Transit service via CTS #854.   Information from 233-3004.
      San Diego Trolley: El Cajon trains. Information 231-
      8549.
Typical business hours: 0800 to 2200 +/-.
Security patrol: No.
Public Rest Rooms: No.   Benches: No.
Restaurants: Both snacks and dining services are available.
Walks and distances: A store-front sidewalk, including three
      short flights of stairs, is 2/10th (.2) of a mile long.

Mall Walking in San Diego County

La Mesa   **Grossmont Shopping Center**

Description: Large shopping center with major department
     stores, air-conditioned food court, an extensive variety of
     shops and a multi-screen theatre.
Located at 5500 Grossmont Center Drive, La Mesa, 92041.
Community/Area name: La Mesa.
Thomas Guide: Page 55, Grid D-6.
Intersection of Interstate 8 and Grossmont Center Drive. Entry
     also possible from Fletcher Parkway.
Transit service via SDT #15. Also via CTS #854, #881, #882,
     #883, #884, #885, #888, #894.   Information 233-3004.
     San Diego Trolley: El Cajon line. Information 231-8549.
Typical business hours: 0900 to 2200 +/-.
Security patrol: Yes.
Public Rest Rooms: Mapped on directory board.   Benches: Yes.
Restaurants: Wide variety in food court, plus fine dining estab-
     lishments on the perimeter of the Center.
Walks and distances: Inside the center; it is 1/4 (.25) mile from
     Bullocks to Focus, and 2/10th (.2) mile from Buffams to
     the directory board at the Center Drive entrance.
To safely walk the building perimeter, which is a 1-1/2 (1.5) mile
     route, go left in order to face traffic on Center Drive
     while walking around the Bullocks' building.
Area walks are not feasible due to heavy traffic.

Mall Walking in San Diego County

La Mesa Crossroads   # La Mesa

Description: A large full-service community shopping center.
Located at 7910 El Cajon Boulevard, La Mesa, 92041.
Community/Area name: La Mesa.
Thomas Guide: Page 62, Grid C-1.
Intersection of El Cajon Boulevard and Baltimore Drive.
Transit service via SDT #15.   Information from 233-3004.
Typical business hours: 0800 to 2200 +/-.
Security patrol: Unknown.
Public Rest Rooms: No.   Benches: No.
Restaurants: A small variety of food service is available.
Walks and distances: A walk around the building perimeter will
        total 3/10th (.3) of a mile.
Area walks are not feasible due to heavy traffic, absence of
        sidewalks and residential sections of restricted access.

Mall Walking in San Diego County

La Mesa

Description: A large, full-service, community shopping center.
Located at 8000 La Mesa Boulevard, La Mesa, 92041.
Community/Area name: La Mesa.
Thomas Guide: Page 62, Grid C-2.
Intersection of University Avenue and Allison Avenue.
Transit service via SDT #7, #15.   Also CTS #854.
 Information from 233-3004.
 San Diego Trolley: El Cajon line. Information 231-8549.
Typical business hours: 0600 to 2400 +/-.
Security patrol: Unknown.
Public Rest Rooms: No.   Benches: No.
Restaurants: An extensive selection of snacks, fast foods and
 dining facilities are available in the center.
Walks and distances: The store-front sidewalk of the largest
 building is 2/10th (.2) of a mile long.
An area walk of one mile begins by exiting onto University
 Avenue and walking left to La Mesa Boulevard. Turn
 left (South-East) and continue up La Mesa to Spring
 Street. Go left (North-East) to Allison Avenue, left again
 to University and left to the point of beginning.

Mall Walking in San Diego County

Lake Murray Village   **La Mesa**

Description: Medium-size shopping center with an excellent
        selection of community services. Was previously known
        as Town & Country Shopping Center.
Located at 5600-5650 Baltimore Drive, La Mesa, 92041.
Community/Area name: La Mesa.
Thomas Guide: Page 55, Grid B-5.
Intersection of Lake Murray Boulevard and Baltimore Drive.
Transit service via SDT #81.   Also CTS #854.
        Information from 233-3004.
Typical business hours: 0600 to 2400 +/-.
Security patrol: Unknown.
Public Rest Rooms: No.   Benches: No.
Restaurants: Snack services available.
Walks and distances: A walk along sidewalks of both structures
        will total 1/4 (.25) of a mile.
A perimeter walk of the structures is not feasible.
Area walks are not feasible due to extensive residential develop-
        ment with restricted access and adjacent streets carry-
        ing heavy traffic.

Mall Walking in San Diego County

La Mesa

Description: A small strip of budget retail outlets in an unnamed
 center now undergoing refurbishing.
Located at 9100 Fletcher Parkway, La Mesa, 92041.
Community/Area name: La Mesa.
Thomas Guide: Page 55, Grid E-4.
Intersection of Fletcher Parkway and Dallas Street.
Transit service not available.
Typical business hours: 0900 to 2100 +/-.
Security patrol: No.
Public Rest Rooms: No.   Benches: No.
Restaurants: Food services are available.
Walks and distances: Suitable for strolling. Perimeter and area
 walks are not feasible.

Mall Walking in San Diego County

Spring Valley Center   **La Presa**

Description: A medium size community shopping center with an
        emphasis on clothing and home furnishings.
Located at 555 Sweetwater Road, National City, 92077.
Community/Area name: La Presa.
Thomas Guide: Page 67, Grid D-2.
Intersection of Sweetwater Road and Jamacha Boulevard.
Transit service via SDT #11. Also CTS #856.
        Information from 233-3004.
Typical business hours: 0700 to 2200 +/-.
Security patrol: Unknown.
Public Rest Rooms: No.   Benches: No.
Restaurants: Snacks and fast-food facilities are available.
Walks and distances: The store-front sidewalks total 4/10th (.4)
        of a mile in length.
A walk around the building perimeter is 8/10th (.8) of a mile.
Area walking is not feasible due to traffic activity and layout of
        adjacent streets. Spring Valley County Park is across
        Jamacha Boulevard. A major swap meet is held near the
        park every weekend.

Mall Walking in San Diego County

Lake San Marcos
Lake Village Center

Description: Small service center for a major North County
    retirement and golf community. A fine walking area.
Located at 1146 San Marino Drive, San Marcos, 92069.
Community/Area name: Lake San Marcos.
Thomas Guide: Page 20, Grid E-2.
Intersection of San Marino Drive and La Bonita Drive.
Transit service via NCTD #341.
    Information from 722- or 743-6283.
Typical business hours: 0900 to 1800 +/-.
Security patrol: Yes.
Public Rest Rooms: Locked. Inquire for a key.   Benches: Yes.
Restaurants: Coffee shop service available.
Walks and distances: A property perimeter walk of 4/10th (.4)
    mile includes sidewalks of San Marino Drive.
The shortest (2-2/10th [.2.2] miles) walk has heavy ups and
    downs. Exit onto San Marino Drive and follow it left to
    Hermosito Drive on your right. Walk up Hermosito to
    Camino del Arroyo, go left (up) to the end, turn around
    and walk back down to Rancho Santa Fe Road. Go right
    to Lake San Marcos Drive, turn right downhill to San
    Marino and go left to the point of beginning.
An excellent longer walk (2-9/10th [2.9] miles) also begins on
    San Marino Drive. Walk right, over the bridge, and con-
    tinue ahead on San Pablo Drive. It loops left to return
    you to the bridge. Watch the signs: There are Drives,
    Courts, Ways. This walk can be reduced to about two
    miles by following San Julian Drive when you find it on
    your left. It rejoins San Pablo Drive past the golf course.

Mall Walking in San Diego County

Marketplace at the Grove   # Lemon Grove

Description: Large multi-service two-level shopping center with
       open mall and theatre.
Located at 3450 College Avenue, San Diego, 92106.
Community/Area name: Lemon Grove.
Thomas Guide: Page 61, Grid F-6.
Intersection of College Avenue and College Grove Drive.
Transit service via SDT #5, #16, #36.   Also CTS #856.
     Information from 233-3004
Typical business hours: 0900 to 2100 +/-.
Security patrol: Yes.
Public Rest Rooms: Mapped on Directory Board.   Benches: Yes.
Restaurants: The small Food Court offers a selection of menus.
Walks and distances: Via the open mall section, it is 3/10th (.3)
       of a mile from the theatre to the J.C. Penney store.
A perimeter walk around the entire structure is 8/10th (.8) of a
       mile.
Area walks are not feasible due to traffic and adjacent freeway.

Mall Walking in San Diego County

Linda Vista

Description: Medium-size community service center including a
    major food chain outlet and a drug store.
Located at 6937 Linda Vista Road, San Diego, 92111.
Community/Area name: Linda Vista.
Thomas Guide: Page 53, Grid B-5.
Intersection of Linda Vista Road and Comstock Street.
Transit service via SDT #4.   Information from 233-3004.
Typical business hours: 0700 to 2200 +/-.
Security patrol: Yes.
Public Rest Rooms: No.   Benches: No.
Restaurants: Snacks and fast food are available.
Walks and distances: A walk around the perimeter of the store
    complex will total 3/10th (.3) of a mile.
Area walking is not recommended.

Mall Walking in San Diego County

Arena Plaza   # Loma Portal

Description: A large center with emphasis on clothing, home fur-
        nishings and remodeling supplies.
Located at 3245 Sports Arena Boulevard, San Diego, 92106.
Community/Area name: Loma Portal.
Thomas Guide: Page 59, Grid E-3.
Intersection of Sports Arena Boulevard and Kemper Street.
Transit service via SDT #6, #9, #34.   Informa-
        tion from 233-3004.
Typical business hours: 0900 to 2100 +/-.
Security patrol: Yes.
Public Rest Rooms: No.   Benches: No.
Restaurants: Snack food is available.
Walks and distances: A perimeter walk of the Ralphs/Target
        building will total 7/10th (.7) of a mile including the
        necessary sidewalk portion of East Drive.
An area walk totals 1-1/2 (1.5) miles. Exit onto Sports Arena
        Boulevard and walk left (North-West) to Kemper Street,
        then go left (South-West) to Midway Drive. Turn left on
        Midway and walk to East Drive, go left to Sports Arena
        Boulevard and continue left to the point of beginning.

Mall Walking in San Diego County

Loma Portal

Description: A shopping center of medium size with emphasis on household furnishings and accessories. A multi-screen theatre and dining services are available.

Located at 3146 Sports Arena Boulevard, San Diego, 92106.

Community/Area name: Loma Portal.

Thomas Guide: Page 59, Grid E-3.

Intersection of Sports Arena Boulevard and Rosecrans Street.

Transit service via SDT #6, #9, #34. Information from 233-3004.

Typical business hours: 1000 to 2200 +/-.

Security patrol: Yes.

Public Rest Rooms: Yes; at East entrance.   Benches: Yes.

Restaurants: Several dinner houses are available.

Walks and distances: Excellent for strolling.

Area walks not feasible due to traffic congestion.

Mall Walking in San Diego County

Loma Square   # Loma Portal

Description: A medium-size center with its emphasis on clothing
    and home furnishings.
Located at 3331 Rosecrans Street, San Diego, 92106.
Community/Area name: Loma Portal.
Thomas Guide: Page 59, Grid E-3.
Intersection of Rosecrans Street and Midway Drive.
Transit service via SDT #6, #9. #34, #35.
    Information from 233-3004.
Typical business hours: 0900 to 2100 +/-.
Security patrol: Unknown.
Public Rest Rooms: No.   Benches: No.
Restaurants: Snack services are available.
Walks and distances: The store-front sidewalk is 1/4 (.25) of a
    mile in length. A walk around the perimeter of the build-
    ing is 6/10th (.6) of a mile.
Area walking is not feasible due to traffic and property location.

Mall Walking in San Diego County

Loma Portal

Description: A small community services center.

Located at 3960-80 West Point Loma Blvd. San Diego, 92106.

Community/Area name: Loma Portal.

Thomas Guide: Page 59, Grid D-3.

Intersection of West Point Loma Boulevard and Groton Street.

Transit service via SDT #6, #34.   Information from 233-3004.

Typical business hours: 0900 to 2100 +/-.

Security patrol: No.

Public Rest Rooms: No.   Benches: No.

Restaurants: Numerous fast-food and ethnic eating places.

Walks and distances: A building perimeter walk will be 4/10th
(.4) of a mile in length.

One block west, on the same side of the street, is Loma Riviera
Drive leading into a group of quiet curving streets.

A 1-7/10th (1.7) miles up/down area walk is across West Point
Loma Boulevard, from Point Loma Plaza. Exit the Plaza
onto Point Loma and walk left to Bob Street. Turn left
(South) and continue to Worden Street, go left (uphill) on
Worden and it soon becomes Leland. Follow Leland
downhill on the left where it changes to Kemper Street.
This brings you to Midway Drive, turn left and go to
Point Loma, then left again to the beginning.

Mall Walking in San Diego County

Point Loma Plaza   # Loma Portal

Description: A medium-size full-service community center.
Located at 3689 Midway Drive, San Diego, 92106.
Community/Area name: Loma Portal.
Thomas Guide: Page 59, Grid E-3.
Intersection of Midway Drive and Kemper Street.
Transit service via SDT #6, #9, #34. Information from 233-3004.
Typical business hours: 0600 to 2400 +/-.
Security patrol: Unknown.
Public Rest Rooms: No.   Benches: Yes.
Restaurants: A good selection of snacks and fast-foods.
Walks and distances: The store-front sidewalk is 2/10th (.2) of a
     mile in length. A perimeter walk of the central structure
     will total 1/2 (.5) mile.
A 1-7/10th (1.7) miles up/down area walk begins by exiting the
     Plaza onto Midway Drive. Go left to Point Loma and
     walk left to Bob Street. Turn left (South) and continue to
     Worden Street, go left (uphill) on Worden and it soon be-
     comes Leland. Follow Leland downhill on the left where
     it changes to Kemper Street. This brings you to Midway
     Drive, walk left to the point of beginning.

Mall Walking in San Diego County

Loma Portal

Description: A small, two-level community center emphasizing
     services of local orientation.
Located at 3555 Rosecrans, San Diego, 92106.
Community/Area name: Loma Portal.
Thomas Guide: Page 59, Grid E-3.
Intersection of Rosecrans Street and Midway Drive.
Transit service via SDT #6, #9, #34. Information from 233-3004.
Typical business hours: 0800 to 1800 +/-.
Security patrol: Unknown.
Public Rest Rooms: No.   Benches: No.
Restaurants: Snacks and deli services are available.
Walks and distances: The store-front sidewalk is 2/10th (.2) of a
     mile in length.
Heavy traffic and commercial activity make area walking not
     feasible.

Mall Walking in San Diego County

Sports Arena Square   # Loma Portal

Description: A small dining and entertainment center adjacent
      to the San Diego Sports Arena. Multi-screen theatre.
Located at 3350 Sports Arena Boulevard, San Diego, 92106.
Community/Area name: Loma Portal.
Thomas Guide: Page 59, Grid E-3.
Intersection of Sports Arena Boulevard and East Drive.
Transit service via SDT #6, #9, #34. Information from 233-3004.
Typical business hours: 0700 to 2200 +/-.
Security patrol: During events at the Sports Arena.
Public Rest Rooms: No.   Benches: No.
Restaurants: Numerous choices of mid-range dining available.
Walks and distances: A walk around the building perimeter will
      total 1/4 (.25) mile. Area walking is not feasible.
The adjacent Sports Arena parking lot, when empty, provides an
      opportunity to practice stride techniques without conflict
      with other pedestrians.

Mall Walking in San Diego County

Loma Portal

Description: A business-oriented community center.
Located at 3740-3760 Sports Arena Blvd., San Diego, 92106.
Community/Area name: Loma Portal.
Thomas Guide: Page 59, Grid D-3.
Intersection of Sports Arena Boulevard and Hancock Street.
Transit service via SDT #6, #9, #34. Information from 233-3004.
Typical business hours: 1000 to 2200 +/-.
Security patrol: Unknown.
Public Rest Rooms: No.   Benches: Yes.
Restaurants: Snacks and several ethnic dining houses.
Walks and distances: A walk around the building perimeter will
        total 4/10th (.4) of a mile.
Area walking is not feasible due to traffic and lack of pathways.

Mall Walking in San Diego County

Flower Hill Mall.   # Lomas Santa Fe

Description: Small, upscale, boutique shopping center with a
        theatre. This is not an enclosed air-conditioned mall.
Located at 2710 Via del Valle, Del Mar, 92014.
Community/Area name: Lomas Santa Fe.
Thomas Guide: Page 30, Grid B-6.
Intersection of Interstate 5 and Via de la Valle.
Parking entry from Via de la Valle or San Andres Drive.
Transit service via NCTD #308.
        Information from 722- or 743-6283.
Typical business hours: 0700 to 2200 +/-.
Security patrol:Unknown.
Public Rest Rooms: No.   Benches: Yes.
Restaurants: Several quality restaurants.
Walks and distances: Store-front sidewalk totals 3/10 (.3) mile.
Building perimeter walk not possible. Area walk not feasible.
Across Via del Valle street is an un-named shopping center with
        fast-food outlets. A 1/2 (.5) mile walk is possible around
        the building perimeter. An area walk is not feasible.

Mall Walking in San Diego County

Lomas Santa Fe

Lomas Santa Fe Plaza

Description: Also known as Plaza of the Four Flags and Lomas
Santa Fe Gardens. This twined shopping complex
provides an upscale community center with a fine
department store and boutique shopping facilities.

Located at 901 Lomas Santa Fe Drive, Solana Beach, 92075.

Community/Area name: Lomas Santa Fe.

Thomas Guide: Page 30, Grid B-4.

Intersection of Interstate 5 and Lomas Santa Fe Drive.

Parking entry from Lomas Santa Fe Drive, Marine View Avenue
or San Andres Drive.

Transit service not available.

Typical business hours: 0700 to 2200 +/-.

Security patrol: Yes.

Public Rest Rooms: No.   Benches: No.

Restaurants: A good selection of quality dining opportunities.

Walks and distances: Store-front sidewalks total 3/10th (.3) mile
for both the Plaza and Gardens. To walk the perimeters
of both complexes will total 7/10th (.7) mile.

An area walk of 8/10th (.8) mile begins by exiting west onto
Marine View Avenue. Turn left (South) to San Andres
Drive, go left (East) to Via Banderas Drive, and left
again (North) up Banderas to Lomas Santa Fe Drive.
Walk left (West) to Marine View. Go left (South) to
beginning. This is a lovely route of up/down walking.

Mall Walking in San Diego County

Mira Mesa Center   **Mira Mesa**

Description: This is a large open shopping center that is also
     known as the Mira Mesa Mall. There are theatres, major
     food outlets, community services, good restaurants and
     several fast food services.
Located at 8294 Mira Mesa Boulevard, San Diego, 92126.
Community/Area name: Mira Mesa.
Thomas Guide: Page 39, Grid E-2.
Intersection of Mira Mesa Boulevard and Camino Ruiz.
Parking entry from Mira Mesa Boulevard, Camino Ruiz and ad-
     jacent side streets.
Transit service via SDT #20A, #30.   Information 233-3004.
Typical business hours: 0800 to 2200 +/-.
Security patrol: Yes.
Public Rest Rooms: No.   Benches: Yes.
Restaurants: An excellent variety of specialty restaurants and
     fast food chain services.
Walks and distances: A sidewalk around the central building
     complex provides 6/10 (.6) mile of walking.
An area walk of 1-4/10 (1.4) miles begins by exiting East onto
     Camino Ruiz. Turn left (North) and walk to Westmore
     Road. Go left (West) to Reagan Road and left (South) to
     Mira Mesa Boulevard. Continue left (East) on Mira Mesa
     to Camino Ruiz, then go left (North) to beginning.

Mall Walking in San Diego County

Mira Mesa

Mira Mesa Square

Description: Medium size community shopping center.
Located at 9326 Mira Mesa Boulevard, San Diego 92126.
Community/Area name: Mira Mesa.
Thomas Guide: Page 40, Grid A-2.
Intersection of Mira Mesa Boulevard and Black Mountain Road.
Transit service via SDT #20, #20A   Information from 233-3004.
Typical business hours: 0900 to 2100 +\-.
Security patrol: Unknown.
Public Rest Rooms: No.   Benches: No.
Restaurants: Several fast-food outlets are in the center.
Walks and distances: A walk around the perimeter of the central
        buildings will total 1/2 (.5) mile.
Area walking is not feasible due to heavy traffic and restricted
        access to the North and East.

Mall Walking in San Diego County

Belmont Park Shopping Center　　　**Mission Beach**

Description: One of San Diego's better places to walk from.
Located at 3126 Mission Boulevard, San Diego, 92109.
Community/Area name: Mission Beach.
Thomas Guide: Page 59, Grid A-1.
Intersection of Mission Beach Blvd. and West Mission Bay Dr.
Transit service via SDT #34, #81.　　Information from 233-3004.
Typical business hours: 0900 to 2100 +/-.
Security patrol: Yes.
Public Rest Rooms: Yes.　　　　　　　　　Benches: Yes.
Restaurants: Both snacks and dining facilities available.
Walks and distances: From Belmont Park, where the roller
　　　　　coaster is, you can use the interesting Bayfront Walk
　　　　　surrounding Mission Bay. Or follow the Ocean Front
　　　　　Walk north about two miles from Mission Bay Channel.
　　　　　A city park is across Mission Boulevard.

Mall Walking in San Diego County

Mission Village

Mission Village Plaza

Description: Medium-size community shopping center with a
   food chain outlet, drug store and post office.
Located at 9190 Gramercy Drive, San Diego, 92123.
Community/Area name: Mission Village.
Thomas Guide: Page 53, Grid F-3.
Intersection of Gramercy Drive and Ruffin Road.
Transit service via SDT #16.   Information from 233-3004.
Typical business hours: 0600 to 2400 +/-.
Security patrol: Unknown.
Public Rest Rooms: No.   Benches: No.
Restaurants: Snack service and restaurants are in the plaza.
Walks and distances: Store-front sidewalks are 3/10th (.3) of a
   mile in length. A building perimeter walk is not feasible.
A one-mile area walk begins on Gramercy Drive. Walk left
   (East) to Ruffin Road and turn left. Continue (North) to
   Village Glen Drive and turn left (West) to Glencollum
   Drive. Angle left on Mobley Street then continue South
   to Gramercy Drive and point of beginning. This is an
   up/down tree-shaded route for residential walking.

Mall Walking in San Diego County

South Bay Plaza   **National City**

Description: A small full-service community shopping center.
Located at 1003 Plaza Boulevard, National City, 92050.
Community/Area name: National City.
Thomas Guide: Page 66, Grid C-5.
Intersection of Place Boulevard and "L" Avenue.
Transit service via SDT #29.   Also NCT #602.
        Information from 233-3004.
Typical business hours: 0800 to 2100 +/-.
Security patrol: Unknown.
Public Rest Rooms: No.   Benches: No.
Restaurants: Snacks and fast foods are available.
Walks and distances: The store-front sidewalk is 2/10th (.2) of a
        mile in length. Perimeter walks are not feasible.
Area walks are not feasible due to traffic and the configuration
        of nearby streets.

Mall Walking in San Diego County

National City

Description: A small strip of local service retailers.
Located at 1727 Sweetwater Road, National City, 92050.
Community/Area name: National City.
Thomas Guide: Page 69, Grid D-2.
Intersection of Sweetwater Road and Prospect Street.
Transit service via NCT #601, #604. Information from 474-7505.
Typical business hours: 0700 to 2100 +/-.
Security patrol: Yes.
Public Rest Rooms: No.   Benches: No.
Restaurants: Fast food and snacks are available
Walks and distances: The store-front sidewalk is 2/10th (.2) of a
    mile in length. A building perimeter walk is not feasible.
An area walk of one mile begins on Sweetwater Road. Walk
    right to Grove Street. Turn right, uphill and follow
    Grove to Vista Way. Go right and continue onto Prospect
    Street which leads downhill into Sweetwater Plaza and
    the beginning. This is a steep up/down walking route.

Mall Walking in San Diego County

Sweetwater Town & Country   **National City**

Description: A large home furnishings and full service com-
          munity shopping center with a major health spa.
Located at 1629 Sweetwater Road, National City, 92050.
Community/Area name: National City.
Thomas Guide: Page 69, Grid D-1.
Intersection of Sweetwater Road and Edgemere Avenue.
Transit service via NCT #601, #605. Information from 474-7505.
Typical business hours: 0600 to 2200 +/-.
Security patrol: Unknown.
Public Rest Rooms: No.   Benches: No.
Restaurants: Sit-down dining, fast foods and snacks are avail-
          able in the center.
Walks and distances: This center is made up of numerous scat-
          tered structures. A perimeter walk around the largest is
          4/10th (.4) of a mile in length.
Adjoining freeways and heavy traffic make area walks difficult.
          For one suggested route, see Sweetwater Plaza which is
          located across the street from Town & Country.

Mall Walking in San Diego County

Nestor

Description: A small community shopping center.
Located at 1690 Palm Avenue, San Diego, 92154.
Community/Area name: Nestor.
Thomas Guide: Page 71, Grid C-4.
Intersection of Palm Avenue and 16th Street.
Transit service via SDT #33, #33A.   Information from 233-3004.
Typical business hours: 0900 to 2200 +/-.
Security patrol: Unknown.
Public Rest Rooms: No.   Benches: No.
Restaurants: Food service and snacks available.
Walks and distances: Suitable for short strolls.

Mall Walking in San Diego County

Camino Town & Country   **Oceanside**

Description: A extensive complex of boutique and large retail
         stores with a multi-screen theatre. To the west, one
         block on Vista Way, is Fire Mountain Center which is a
         small community service plaza.
Located at 2255 El Camino Real, Oceanside, 92054.
Community/Area name: Oceanside.
Thomas Guide: Page 14, Grid B-1.
Intersection of El Camino Real and Vista Way.
Transit service via NCTD #309, #316.   Informa-
         tion from 722- or 643-6283.
Typical business hours: 0900 to 2200 +/-.
Security patrol: Yes.
Public Rest Rooms: No.   Benches: No.
Restaurants: A good variety of eateries and fast food outlets are
         in the two centers.
Walks and distances: Camino T & C, and Fire Mountain, are
         best for strolling. Perimeter or area walks are limited to
         exiting either center onto Vista Way. Walk left to El
         Camino Real and turn left, uphill, toward Via Los Rosas.
         At Los Rosas go left (West) to Via Esmarca, turn left and
         continue to Vista Way and the point of beginning. This is
         1-3/4 (1.75) miles with some up/down walking.

Mall Walking in San Diego County

Oceanside

Description: Small service and office building center behind
      which is an industrial area.
Located at 3400 Mission Avenue, Oceanside, 92054.
Community/Area name: Oceanside.
Thomas Guide: Page 10, Grid A-3.
Intersection of Mission Avenue and Copperwood Way.
Parking entry from Mission Avenue or Copperwood Way.
Transit service via NCTD #303, #313.
      Information from 722- or 743-6283.
Typical business hours: 0900 to 1900 +/-.
Security patrol: Unknown.
Public Rest Rooms: No.   Benches: No.
Restaurants: Several small food services are available.
Walks and distances: Suitable for strolling. Industrial complex
      behind the center makes area walking not feasible.

Mall Walking in San Diego County

El Camino North   **Oceanside**

Description: Three strip centers including Carousel Square, with
    a theatre and complete selection of community services.
Located at 2657 Vista Way, Oceanside, 92054.
Community/Area name: Oceanside.
Thomas Guide: Page 14, Grid A-2.
Intersection of Vista Way and Via Esmarca.
Transit service via NCTD #309, #316.
        Information from 722- or 743-6283.
Typical business hours: 1000 to 2200 +/-.
Security patrol: Yes.
Public Rest Rooms: No.   Benches: No.
Restaurants: A wide selection of dining services including fast
    food outlets, snack bars and a diet-menu house.
Walks and distances: The combination of store-front sidewalks,
    from East to West, is one mile.
A long walk of 2-6/10 (2.6) miles begins at the doorway of Spoons
    Restaurant at the East end. Walk West on the several
    store-front sidewalks to Entry Drive. Go right (North) a
    short distance to Vista Way and turn right. Follow Vista
    Way to the signed entry drive into El Camino North. Go
    right to the theatre then left to the point of beginning.

Mall Walking in San Diego County

Oceanside

Description: A small service center for the adjoining Oceanside
retirement community of Oceana.
Located at 500 Vista Bello (Vista Campana), Oceanside, 92054.
Community/Area name: Oceanside.
Thomas Guide: Page 10, Grid A-3.
Intersection of Via Oceana and Vista Bello (Vista Campana).
Parking entry from Vista Bello (Via Campana).
Transit service via NCTD #309.
Information from 722- or 743-6283.
Typical business hours: 0900 to 1800 +/-.
Security patrol: Unknown.
Public Rest Rooms: No.   Benches: No.
Restaurants: Cafe open from 0700.
Walks and distances: There is a fine 1-2/10th (1.2) miles loop
walk on Vista Campana. Exit the Mercado onto Vista
Bello and walk right (South) to Vista Campana. Con-
tinue ahead on Vista Campana which curves gently to
the left. There are several view points with benches mid-
way on the tree-shaded walk. Where Vista Campana
returns to Vista Bello, go left to the point of beginning.

Mall Walking in San Diego County

Mission Square   # Oceanside

Description: A refurbished full-service shopping center adjacent
   to the downtown area and Interstate 8.
Located at 1000 Mission Avenue, Oceanside, 92054.
Community/Area name: Oceanside.
Thomas Guide: Page 9, Grid C-5.
Intersection of Mission Avenue and Horne Street.
Parking entry from Mission Avenue or Horne Street.
Transit service via NCTD #303, #313.
   Information from 722- or 743-6283.
Typical business hours: 0800 to 2200 +/-.
Security patrol: Unknown.
Public Rest Rooms: No.   Benches: No.
Restaurants: Several fast food outlets.
Walks and distances: Suitable for strolling. Building or area
   perimeter walks not recommended.
This shopping center is about one-half mile from the beach. Exit
   onto Mission Avenue and walk right, downhill, facing
   the Pacific ocean for beach or boardwalk ventures.

Mall Walking in San Diego County

Oceanside

Description: A small community services and food center.
Located at 2000 Mission Avenue, Oceanside, 92054.
Community/Area name: Oceanside.
Thomas Guide: Page 9, Grid D-5.
Intersection of Mission Avenue and Canyon Drive.
Parking entry from Canyon Drive or Mission Avenue.
Transit service via NCTD #316, #318.
Information from 722- or 743-6283.
Typical business hours: 0800 to 2200 +/-.
Security patrol: Unknown.
Public Rest Rooms: No.   Benches: Yes.
Restaurants: Fast food available.
Walks and distances: The store-front sidewalk is 2/10th (.2) mile
in length and suitable for strolling.
Walking the building perimeter or property area is not recom-
mended.

Mall Walking in San Diego County

Oceanside Town & Country   **Oceanside**

Description: A collection of shopping centers extending along
      Oceanside Boulevard; also known as Oceanside Five.
Located at 1701 Oceanside Boulevard, Oceanside, 92054.
Community/Area name: Oceanside
Thomas Guide: Page 13, Grid E-1.
Intersection of Interstate 5 and Oceanside Boulevard.
Transit service via NCTD #316, #318.
      Information from 722- or 743-6283.
Typical business hours: 0800 to 2200 +/-.
Security patrol: Unknown.
Public Rest Rooms: No.   Benches: No.
Restaurants: Several places to eat are in the complex.
Walks and distances: Suitable for strolling. Building perimeter
      and area walks not recommended because of heavy traf-
      fic and adjacent industrial/commercial activity.

Mall Walking in San Diego County

Oceanside

Tri-City Crossroads

Description: A medium-size strip shopping center.

Located at 3817 Plaza Drive, Oceanside, 92054.

Community/Area name: Oceanside.

Thomas Guide: Page 14, Grid E-2.

Intersection of Plaza Drive and Freeway 78 Offramp.

Transit service via NCTD #311.

      Information from 722- or 743-6283.

Typical business hours: 0700 to 2200 +/-.

Security patrol: Unknown.

Public Rest Rooms: No.   Benches: No.

Restaurants: A wide variety of fast food and snack sources.

Walks and distances: A building perimeter walk is 2/3rd (.65) of a mile. The front sidewalk is 1/3rd (.3) mile long.

Area walking is not recommended due to incomplete construction of planned roadways and sidewalks.

Mall Walking in San Diego County

Pacific Plaza I and II   **Pacific Beach**

Description: Medium-size shopping centers in two units of strip
        retailers and community services. Across Jewell Street is
        another center with additional services.
Located at 1700-1800 Garnet Avenue, San Diego, 92109.
Community/Area name: Pacific Beach.
Thomas Guide: Page 52, Grid C-3.
Intersection of Garnet Ave., Ingraham Street and Lamont St.
Transit service via SDT #27.   Information from 233-3004.
Typical business hours: 0800 to 2200 +/-.
Security patrol: Yes.
Public Rest Rooms: No.   Benches: No.
Restaurants: A number of fast-food and mid-range restaurant
        services are available in the Plazas.
Walks and distances: A building perimeter walk of the largest
        central section will total 1/2 (.5) mile.
An area walk of 1-1/10th (.1.1) miles begins on Garnet Avenue.
        Go left (East) to Lamont Street and turn left (North) to
        Diamond Street. Walk left (West) on Diamond to In-
        graham Street and turn left. Continue South to Garnet
        and walk left to the point of beginning.

Mall Walking in San Diego County

Pacific Beach

The Promenade

Description: A pleasing two-level shopping center with upscale
  boutique stores and limited community services.
Located at 4150 Mission Boulevard, San Diego, 92109.
Community/Area name: Pacific Beach.
Thomas Guide: Page 52, Grid A-5.
Intersection of Mission Boulevard and Pacific Beach Drive.
Transit service via SDT #34, #81.   Information from 233-3004.
Typical business hours: 1000 to 2200 +/-.
Security Patrol: Unknown.   Benches: Yes.
Public Rest Rooms: City rest rooms are on Pacific Beach Drive
  which is at the South end of The Promenade.
Restaurants: Both dining and snack services are available.
Walks and distances: The Ocean Front Walk is one-half block to
  the West on which walks of several miles are possible.
  The beach and Pacific ocean are accessed from the Walk.
  Across Mission Boulevard is Bonita Cove and a large
  public park with a number of fine paved foot paths.

Mall Walking in San Diego County

Palm Plaza   **Palm City**

Description: Small and busy community shopping center.
Located at 3350 Palm Avenue, San Diego, 92154.
Community/Area name: Palm City.
Thomas Guide: Page 71, Grid F-4.
Intersection of Palm Avenue and Beyer Way (Picador Blvd.).
Transit service via SDT #33, #33A.   Information from 233-3004.
Typical business hours: 0700 to 2200 +/-.
Security patrol: Unknown.
Public Rest Rooms: No.   Benches: No.
Restaurants: Food service and snacks available.
Walks and distances: Useful for short strolls in the center. Area
    walking not recommended due to heavy traffic.

Mall Walking in San Diego County

Poway

Description: Full service community shopping center with the
Pomerado Plaza Center on adjoining property.
Located at 12200 Poway Road, Poway, 92064.
Community/Area name: Poway.
Thomas Guide: Page 36, Grid F-4.
Intersection of Poway Road and Pomerado Road.
Parking entry from Pomerado Road or Poway Road.
Transit service via CTS #844, #845. Information from 233-3004.
Typical business hours: 0700 to 2300 +/-.
Security patrol: Unknown.
Public Rest Rooms: No.   Benches: No.
Restaurants: A broad variety of mid-range dining houses.
Walks and distances: Store-front sidewalks are 3/10th (.3) of a
mile in length. A walk around the perimeter of the main
structure totals 8/10th (.8) of a mile.
Local terrain makes area walks not recommended.
Pomerado Plaza is adjacent on the west with an additional
selection of stores and food services. Excellent for stroll-
ing but area walks not feasible.

Mall Walking in San Diego County

Twin Peaks Plaza   **Poway**

Description: A medium-size full-service community shopping
       center with a wide selection of services.
Located at 14823 Pomerado Road, Poway, 92064.
Community/Area name: Poway.
Thomas Guide: Page 32, Grid F-6.
Intersection of Twin Peaks Road (Camino del Norte) and
       Pomerado Road.
Transit service via CTS #843, #844, #845.
       Information from 233-3004.
Typical business hours: 0900 to 2100 +/-.
Security patrol: Unknown.
Public Rest Rooms: No.   Benches: No.
Restaurants: A wide variety of food services are available.
Walks and distances: A store-front walk totals 2/10th (.2) mile. A
       building perimeter walk is 1/2 (.5) mile.
An up/down walk in the area is 9/10th (.9) mile. Exit Twin Peaks
       Plaza onto Pomerado Road, walk left (South) to Route 56
       (a side street) and turn left. Follow Route 56 uphill
       (North-East) to Twin Peaks Road, walk left downhill to
       Pomerado. Go left again to the point of beginning.

Mall Walking in San Diego County

Rancho Bernardo

Description: The largest of three adjoining shopping centers in-
cluding The Plaza and The Town Center.
Located at 11950 Bernardo Plaza Dr., Rancho Bernardo, 92128.
Community/Area name: Rancho Bernardo.
Thomas Guide: Page 32, Grid E-1.
Intersection of Bernardo Center Drive and Bernardo Plaza Dr.
Transit service via SDT #20, #20C.   Information from 233-3004.
Typical business hours: 0800 to 2200 +/-.
Security patrol: Yes.
Public Rest Rooms: No.   Benches: Yes.
Restaurants: Wide variety of fine dining, fast food and snack
services are available among the three centers.
Walks and distances: The building perimeter of the Town Center
provides a walk of one mile.
A 1-1/3rd (1.3) mile area walk begins on Bernardo Center Drive.
Walk left (South) to Lomica Drive then turn left (East)
and continue to Acena Drive. Go left (North) to Rancho
Bernardo Drive, left again (West) to Bernardo Center
Drive and continue left to point of beginning.

Mall Walking in San Diego County

Rancho Bernardo Village   **Rancho Bernardo**

Description: Small community shopping center with full serv-
     ices, also known as Pomerado Village.
Located at 12449 Rancho Bernardo Rd, Rancho Bernardo, 92128
Community/Area name: Rancho Bernardo.
Thomas Guide: Page 32, Grid F-2.
Intersection of Rancho Bernardo Road and Pomerado Road.
Transit service via SDT #20, #20C. Information from 233-3004.
     Also via CTS #844, #845.   Information from 233-3004.
Typical business hours: 0800 to 2100 +/-.
Security patrol: Unknown.
Public Rest Rooms: No.   Benches: No.
Restaurants: Several small food services are in the center.
Walks and distances: Strolling recommended. A building
     perimeter walk is not recommended.
A 1-2/10th (1.2) mile area walk begins by exiting onto Rancho
     Bernardo Drive. Turn left (West) and continue to Ber-
     nardo Oaks Drive. Go left (South) on Bernardo Oaks to
     Rios Road, then left (East) to Pomerado Road. Walk left
     (North) to Rancho Bernardo Drive then left again to the
     point of beginning.

Mall Walking in San Diego County

Rancho Bernardo

Description: An attractive upscale boutique shopping center.
Located at 16450 Bernardo Center Dr., Rancho Bernardo, 92128.
Community/Area name: Rancho Bernardo.
Thomas Guide: Page 32, Grid E-1.
Intersection of Rancho Bernardo Road and Bernardo Center
      Drive. Adjacent to Interstate 15 on the West.
Transit service via SDT #20, #20C. Information from 233-3004.
      Also CTS #844.   Information from 233-3004.
Typical business hours: 0900 to 2100 +/-.
Security patrol: Unknown.
Public Rest Rooms: No.   Benches: No.
Restaurants: An excellent variety of food services is available.
Walks and distances: The store-front sidewalk is 3/10th (.3) mile
      long. A perimeter walk of the buildings is not feasible.
A pleasant residential area walk is 1-3/10th (1.3) miles long.
      Exit the Mercado onto Bernardo Center Drive and walk
      left. Look for Bajada Road across the street on your
      right. Follow Bajada (East) as it curves to Graciosa on
      your left. Follow Graciosa (North-West) and it will
      return you to Bernardo Center Drive. Continue left to
      point of beginning. There is some up/down walking on
      this tour.

Mall Walking in San Diego County

Westwood Shopping Center　　　　**Rancho Bernardo**

Description: Small full-service community shopping center.
Located at 11655 Duenda Road (Bernardo Center Drive),
　　　　Rancho Bernardo, 92128.
Community/Area name: Rancho Bernardo.
Thomas Guide: Page 27, Grid E-6.
Intersection of West Bernardo Drive and Duenda Road
　　　　(Bernardo Center Drive).
Transit service via SDT #20, #20C.　Information from 233-3004.
Typical business hours: 0700 to 2200 +/-.
Security patrol: No.
Public Rest Rooms: No.　　　　　　　　　　　　Benches: No.
Restaurants: Snack foods are available.
Walks and distances: A walk around the building perimeter to-
　　　　tals 3/10th (.3) mile.
A somewhat hilly, but attractive, walk of two miles begins on
　　　　West Bernardo Drive. Walk left (South) to Matinal Road
　　　　on the West side of the street. Cross over and follow
　　　　Matinal Road (West) to Matinal Circle on the right. Turn
　　　　right (North) and continue on Matinal Circle to Duenda
　　　　Road, go right (South-East) on Duenda to West Bernardo
　　　　Drive and the point of beginning.

Mall Walking in San Diego County

Rancho Penasquitos

Plaza Rancho Penasquitos

Description: Medium size community shopping center.
Located at 9909 Carmel Mountain Rd, R'cho Penasquitos, 92129
Community/Area name: Rancho Penasquitos.
Thomas Guide: Page 36, Grid B-3.
Intersection of Rancho Penasquitos Boulevard and Carmel
     Mountain Road.
Transit service via SDT #20, #20B. Information from 233-3004.
     Also via CTS #844.   Information from 233-3004.
Typical business hours: 0700 to 2200 +/-.
Security patrol: Unknown.
Public Rest Rooms: No.   Benches: No.
Restaurants: There are several small establishments for food.
Walks and distances: The store-front sidewalk is 3/10th (.3) mile
     long. The building perimeter is a 6/10 (.6) mile walk.
A residential walk of 9/10th (.9) mile begins on Carmel Moun-
     tain Road. Go left (South) to Rancho Penasquitos
     Boulevard then turn right (North-West) uphill with Car-
     mel Mountain Road. At Paseo Montalban go right
     (North-East) to Paseo Cardiel. Turn right (downhill) and
     continue to Carmel Mountain Road and beginning point.

Mall Walking in San Diego County

Campus Plaza   **Rolando**

Description: A medium size, full-service, shopping center
Located at 6155 El Cajon Boulevard, San Diego, 92115.
Community/Area name: Rolando.
Thomas Guide: Page 61, Grid E-2.
Intersection of El Cajon Boulevard and College Avenue.
Transit service via SDT #15, #115.   Information from 233-3004.
Typical business hours: 0600 to 2400 +/-.
Security patrol:Yes.
Public Rest Rooms: No.   Benches: No.
Restaurants: Snacks and fast food services are available.
Walks and distances: The store-front sidewalk is 3/10th (.3) of a
        mile long. A walk around the building perimeter is pos-
        sible. It totals 7/10th (.7) of a mile.
An area walk of 8/10th (.8) mile begins by exiting onto College
        Avenue and turning left. Walk to Acorn Street, go left
        (East) to 62nd Street, turn left (North) on 62nd to El
        Cajon. Go left (South West) to College and beginning.

Mall Walking in San Diego County

Sabre Springs

Sabre Springs Marketplace

Description: A small community shopping center under construction in early 1991. It is adjacent to Poway.
Located at 12630 Sabre Springs Parkway, San Diego, 92128.
Community/Area name: Sabre Springs; west of Poway.
Thomas Guide: Page 36, Grid C-4.
Intersection of Poway Road and Sabre Springs Parkway.
Parking entry from Sabre Springs Parkway.
Transit service via CTS #820, #844.   Information: 233-3004.
Typical business hours: A new center, hours unknown.
Security patrol: Unknown.
Public Rest Rooms: See walking notations.
Benches: In walking areas.
Restaurants: A new center, services unknown.
Walks and distances: Store-front sidewalk, Est. at 3/10 mile.
An excellent area walk of 9/10 (.9) mile begins by exiting onto
Sabre Springs Parkway. Walk left (North) and continue past a small community park with benches to Evening Creek Drive. Go right (East) up Evening Creek to a large community park with public restrooms. On the right (South) are paved paths leading to a downward incline return to Sabre Springs Parkway. Continue ahead (South) to point of beginning.

Mall Walking in San Diego County

Big Bear   **San Carlos**

Description: A medium size complex of two centers, one known
     as San Carlos Shopping Center, joined by narrow alleys.
Located at 7403 Jackson Drive, San Diego, 92119.
Community/Area name: San Carlos.
Thomas Guide: Page 55, Grid A-3.
Intersection of Navajo Road and Jackson Drive.
Transit service via SDT #115.   Information from 233-3004.
Typical business hours: 0800 to 2200 +/-.
Security patrol: Unknown.
Public Rest Rooms: No.   Benches: No.
Restaurants: Fast foods and snacks are available.
Walks and distances: A perimeter walk of the food store complex
     will total 4/10th (.4) of a mile.
A 1-1/10th (1.1) mile up/down area walk begins by exiting onto
     Jackson Drive. Turn left and walk to Golfcrest Drive and
     go left (North) to Navajo Road. Go left uphill to Jackson
     and left again to the point of beginning.

Mall Walking in San Diego County

San Diego

Description: A major shopping facility with a number of fine
 department stores and an extensive selection of small
 retailers with upscale merchandise.
Located at 352 Fashion Valley, San Diego, 92101.
Community/Area name: Mission Valley.
Thomas Guide: Page 60, Grid C-1.
Intersection of Friars Road and Fashion Valley Road.
Transit service via SDT #6, #16, #20, #25, #41, #43, #81.
 Information from 233-3004.
Typical business hours: 1000 to 2100 +/-.
Security patrol: Yes.
Public Rest Rooms: Inquire of fast-food outlets.   Benches: Yes.
Restaurants: A wide variety of food services are available.
Walks and distances: The open air central "mall" is 4/10th (.4) of
 a mile from Robinsons to J.C.Penney.
To walk around the central building perimeter is about 1-1/4
 (1.25) miles depending on your selection of route.
Area walking is not recommended due to heavy traffic and ad-
 jacency to freeways.

Mall Walking in San Diego County

Mission Valley Center   **San Diego**

Description: A large shopping center with major department
         stores and a wide selection of community retailers.
Located at 1702 Camino del Rio North, San Diego, 92101.
Community/Area name: Mission Valley.
Thomas Guide: Page 60, Grid D-1.
Intersection of Camino del Rio North and Mission Center Road.
Transit service via SDT #6, #16, #25, #43, #81.   In-
         formation from 233-3004.
Typical business hours: 1000 to 2100 +/-.
Security patrol: Yes.
Public Rest Rooms: Mapped on Directory Board.   Benches: Yes.
Restaurants: Snacks and fast foods are available.
Walks and distances: The longest open hallway, from the May
         Co. to Wards, is 3/10th (.3) of a mile long.
A perimeter walk is not feasible due to interference by drives
         into an underground garage. Area walks are not recom-
         mended due to heavy traffic and lack of sidewalks.

Mall Walking in San Diego County

San Diego

Description: A small center featuring home furnishings and
medium-price clothing.

Located at 5010 Mission Center Road, San Diego, 92101.

Community/Area name: Mission Valley.

Thomas Guide: Page 60, Grid D-2.

Intersection of Mission Valley Road and Camino de la Reina.

Transit service via SDT #6, #16, #25, #43, #81.　　　Information from 233-3004.

Typical business hours: 1000 to 2100 +/-.

Security patrol: Yes.

Public Rest Rooms: No.　　　　　　　　　　Benches: Yes.

Restaurants: Snack services are available in the center.

Walks and distances: A perimeter walk around the central
building is 4/10th (.4) of a mile in length.

Area walking is not feasible due to heavy traffic, lack of
sidewalks and adjacency to busy freeways.

Mall Walking in San Diego County

Mission Center **San Luis Rey**

Description: A large full-service community shopping center a
mile from the San Luis Rey Mission.

Located at 3700 Mission Avenue, San Luis Rey, 92068.

Community/Area name: San Luis Rey.

Thomas Guide: Page 10, Grid A-3.

Intersection of Mission Avenue and El Camino Real.

Parking entry from Mission Avenue, El Camino Real or Los Arbolitos Boulevard.

Transit service via NCTD #303, #309.

Information from 722- or 743-6283.

Typical business hours: 0600 to 2400 +/-.

Security patrol: Unknown.

Public Rest Rooms: No. Benches: No.

Restaurants: A variety of mid-range dining, fast food and snack
services are available in the Center.

Walks and distances: The store-front sidewalk is 1/4 (.25) mile
long. A building perimeter walk is not recommended.

A 1-1/3rd (1.3) mile area walk passes a small city park with
benches. Exit onto Mission Avenue and turn left. Walk
(East) to El Camino Real, go left (North) to Los Arbolitos
Boulevard. Turn left and follow Los Arbolitos (West) to
Fireside Street. Walk left, with Fireside Park on the
right, to Mission Avenue. Go left to point of beginning.

Mall Walking in San Diego County

San Luis Rey

Description: A long strip of community services and food outlets
about one mile west of San Luis Rey Mission.
Located at 3800 Mission Avenue, San Luis Rey, 92068.
Community/Area name: San Luis Rey.
Thomas Guide: Page 10, Grid B-3.
Intersection of El Camino Real and Mission Avenue.
Parking entry from El Camino Real or Mission Avenue.
Transit service via NCTD #303, #309.
Information from 722- or 743-6283.
Typical business hours: 0800 to 2200 +/-.
Security patrol: Unknown.
Public Rest Rooms: No.   Benches: No.
Restaurants: Snacks, fast food and mid-range dining services.
Walks and distances: Store-front sidewalk is 7/10th (.7) mile.
A perimeter walk of the buildings or surrounding area is not
feasible. San Luis Rey Mission, about one-mile east, in-
volves walking along heavily traveled Mission Avenue.

Mall Walking in San Diego County

Old California   # San Marcos

Description: Though not a shopping center, this complex of 12
      restaurants offers fine opportunities for walking.
Located at 1000 West San Marcos Blvd, San Marcos, 92069.
Community/Area name: San Marcos.
Thomas Guide: Page 21, Grid B-1.
Intersection of West San Marcos Boulevard and Via Vera Cruz.
Transit service via NCTD #341.
            Information from 722- or 743-6283.
Typical business hours: 0700 to 2300 +/-.
Security patrol: Unknown.
Public Rest Rooms: No.   Benches: Yes.
Restaurants: A unique collection of 12 fine restaurants offering
      an unduplicated selection of menus and cuisines.
Walks and distances: It is a 3/10th (.3) mile walk around the
      central building complex.
A level walk of 2 miles begins by exiting onto San Marcos
      Boulevard. Walk left (East) to Via Vera Cruz, turn left
      (North) and continue to Linda Vista Drive. Go left (West)
      and walk to Pacific Street, turn left and follow Pacific to
      San Marcos Boulevard. Turn left and continue to the
      point of beginning in Old California.

Mall Walking in San Diego County

San Marcos

Palomar Plaza

Description: Small full-service community shopping center.
Located at 762 South Rancho Santa Fe Rd, San Marcos, 92069.
Community/Area name: San Marcos.
Thomas Guide: Page 20, Grid F-1.
Intersection of Rancho St. Fe Road and San Marcos Boulevard.
Transit service via NCTD #304, #341.
    Information from 722- or 743-6283.
Typical business hours: 0600 to 2400 +/-.
Security patrol: No.
Public Rest Rooms: No.   Benches: No.
Restaurants: One, plus several snack outlets.
Walks and distances: It is 6/10th (.6) mile around the buildings.
Area walking is limited by adjacent residential properties with
        restricted access. See Rancho San Marcos Village, which
        is across the street, for a fine area walking route.

Mall Walking in San Diego County

Rancho San Marcos Village **San Marcos**

Description: Small full-service community shopping center.
Located at 671 South Rancho Santa Fe Rd, San Marcos, 92069.
Community/Area name: San Marcos.
Thomas Guide: Page 20, Grid F-1.
Intersection of San Marcos Boulevard and Rancho St. Fe Road.
Transit service via NCTD #304, #341.
Information from 722- or 743-6283.
Typical business hours: 0600 to 2400 +/-.
Security patrol: No.
Public Rest Rooms: No.   Benches: No.
Restaurants: There are several fast food outlets and eateries.
Walks and distances: A building perimeter walk totals 2/10th
        (.2) of a mile.
An area walk of 2-1/10th (2.1) miles includes the William Brad-
        ley Community Park. Exit onto San Marcos Boulevard
        and walk left (East) to Pacific Street. Turn left (North)
        and follow Pacific to Linda Vista Drive. Bradley Park is
        on the left. Go left (West) on Linda Vista to Rancho
        Santa Fe Road. Walk left (South) to San Marcos
        Boulevard, then left to the point of beginning.

Mall Walking in San Diego County

San Marcos

San Marcos Village Shopping Center

Description: A small limited-service shopping strip.
Located at 121 South Rancho Santa Fe Rd, San Marcos, 92069.
Community/Area name: San Marcos.
Thomas Guide: Page 16, Grid A-5.
Intersection of South Rancho St. Fe Rd. and Grand Avenue.
Transit service via NCTD #304, #341.
> Information from 722- or 743-6283.
Typical business hours: 0800 to 2200+/-.
Security patrol: No.
Public Rest Rooms: No.   Benches: No.
Restaurants: Several fast-food services and a deli.
Walks and distances: The building perimeter is a 1/2 (.5) mile
> walk. Commercial and industrial activity in the area
> makes area walking not recommended.

Mall Walking in San Diego County

Santee Shopping Center   **Santee**

Description: A small, limited-service, shopping center.
Located at 9365 Mission Gorge Road, Santee, 92071.
Community/Area name: Santee.
Thomas Guide: Page 47, Grid F-5.
Intersection of Mission Gorge Road and Olive Lane.
Transit service via CTS #846, #847, #854.   Infor-
     mation from 233-3004.
Typical business hours: 0900 to 2100 +/-.
Security patrol: No.
Public Rest Rooms: No.   Benches: No.
Restaurants: Snacks and fast food are available.
Walks and distances: Suitable for strolling.
Building parameter and area walks are not feasible.

Mall Walking in San Diego County

San Ysidro

San Diego Factory Outlet Center

Description: A unique medium-size shopping center in which
most stores sell branded "seconds", or damaged-package
merchandise, at substantial discounts.
Located at 4498 Camino de la Plaza, San Diego, 92073.
Community/Area name: San Ysidro.
Thomas Guide: Page 74, Grid C-5.
Intersection of Interstate 5 and "Last U.S. Exit".
Parking is off Camino de la Plaza at Louisiana Street.
Transit service via MTS #932.   Information from 233-3004.
Also via SD Trolley to San Ysidro with a two block walk.
Typical business hours: 1000 to 2100 +/-.
Security patrol: Yes.
Public Rest Rooms: Yes.   Benches: Yes.
Restaurants: A good variety of economy-priced eateries.
Walks and distances: Suitable for Center strolls. Area or
perimeter walking not recommended. This center is
about one block north of the border with Mexico.

Mall Walking in San Diego County

Scripps Marshall's Plaza   # Scripps Miramar Ranch

Description: A large two-section shopping center divided by
        Hibert Street.
Located at 9909 Mira Mesa Boulevard, San Diego, 92131.
Community/Area name: Scripps Miramar Ranch.
Thomas Guide: Page 40, Grid B-2.
Intersection of Mira Mesa Boulevard, Hibert Street and Scripps
        Ranch Boulevard.
Transit service via SDT #20, #20A.   Information from 233-3004.
Typical business hours: 0700 to 2100 +/-.
Security patrol: Yes.
Public Rest Rooms: No.   Benches: No.
Restaurants: A wide variety of fast food and dining estab-
        lishment including fine oriental.
Walks and distances: The smaller shopping center on the West
        is suitable for strolling. The frontage sidewalk is 2/10th
        (.2) of a mile long.
The perimeter of the large center, on the East, totals 1/2 (.5)
        mile around the center building.
A pleasant area walk of 9/10th (.9) mile begins by exiting onto
        Hibert Street, walking left (South) to Treena Street and
        continuing on Treena. The primitive area ahead is a part
        of the Miramar Dam complex. At Scripps Lake Drive go
        left (East) to Scripps Ranch Boulevard and turn left. Fol-
        low Scripps Ranch (North) to Mira Mesa Boulevard, turn
        left (West) and continue to Hibert. Walk left up Hibert to
        the point of beginning.

Mall Walking in San Diego County

Serra Mesa

Description: A medium-size full service strip shopping center
with several food services.
Located at 3200 Greyling Drive, San Diego, 92123.
Community/Area name: Serra Mesa.
Thomas Guide: Page 53, Grid E-3.
Intersection of Sandrock Street and Greyling Drive.
Transit service via SDT #16.   Information from 233-3004.
Typical business hours: 0700 to 2300 +/-.
Security patrol: Unknown.
Public Rest Rooms: No.   Benches: No.
Restaurants: Snack service and dining houses are in the center.
Walks and distances: The perimeter of the main building and its
sidewalks total 4/10th (.4) of a mile.
Begin an easy 9/10th (.9) mile area walk by exiting the parking
lot North onto Sandrock Street. Turn left (North) to
Murray Ridge Road. Go left (South) on Murray Ridge to
Pinecrest Avenue, and left (East) to Greyling Drive.
Walk left to Sandrock Street and point of beginning.

Mall Walking in San Diego County

Solana Beach Towne Centre   # Solana Beach

Description: This is a complex of three full-service community
        shopping centers separated by Solana Hills Drive.
Located at 689 Lomas Santa Fe Drive, Solana Beach, 92075.
Community/Area name: Solana Beach.
Thomas Guide: Page 30, Grid A-4.
Intersection of Lomas Santa Fe Drive and Solana Hills Drive.
Parking entry from Solana Hills Drive or Lomas Santa Fe Drive.
Transit service via NCTD #308.
        Information from 722- or 743-6283.
Typical business hours: 0600 to 2400 +/-.
Security patrol: Yes.
Public Rest Rooms: No.   Benches: No.
Restaurants: A selection of fast-food services.
Walks and distances: A walk around all buildings of the smaller
        center is 2/10th (.2) mile. The perimeter of buildings in
        either the Dixieline or Marshall's center is 1/2 (.5) mile.
An area walk of 6/10th (.6) mile from the larger center begins
        with exiting onto Solana Hills Drive. Go left (North) to
        Lomas Santa Fe Drive and turn left. Continue west to
        Stevens Avenue then left (South) on Stevens. Walk to
        San Rodolfo Drive, go left again (East) and continue on
        San Rodolfo to Solana Hills Drive and beginning.

Mall Walking in San Diego County

Temecula, Riverside   Rancho California Town Center

Description: A major full-service community shopping center
    with a multi-screen theatre and office building.
Address: 27450 Ynez Road, Temecula, California 92390.
Community/Area name: Rancho California.
Thomas Guide: Page 125, Riverside County.
Intersection of Rancho California Road and Ynez Road.
Transit service via Greyhound. Two busses daily from San Diego
    via Escondido.   Information from 239-9171.
Typical business hours: 0900 to 2200 +/-.
Security patrol: Yes.
Public Rest Rooms: No.   Benches: No.
Restaurants: A wide variety of dining choices are available.
Walks and distances: It is 1/4 (.25) of a mile around the smaller
    complex anchored by PC Computer and SubMariner.
It is 1/2 (.5) mile around the larger complex which has Savon
    and Petoc as the corner stores.
A walk around the theatre/Target complex is 7/10th (.7) of a
    mile. Behind the building use the up/down entry drive
    off Rancho California Road as a portion of the route.
    Area walking is not feasible.

Mall Walking in San Diego County

Costa Verde   # University City

Description: A large upscale boutique, food outlet and com-
  munity service center on two levels. Underground garage
  parking is available.
Located at 8700 Genesee Avenue, San Diego, 92122.
Community/Area name: University City.
Thomas Guide: Page 44, Grid E-2.
Intersection of Genesee Avenue and La Jolla Village Drive.
Parking entry from Genesee Avenue, Las Palmas or LJ Drive.
Transit service via SDT #30, #34, #34A, #41, #50, #105.
  Information from 233-3004.
  Also NCTD #301. Information from 722- or 743-6283.
Typical business hours: 1000 to 2100 +/-.
Security patrol: Yes. Escalators and an elevator are available.
Public Rest Rooms: Mapped on Directory Board.   Benches: Yes
Restaurants: A variety of specialty food sources and snacks.
Walks and distances: The loop road in and around the property
  is 7/10 (.7) miles in length.
An area walking tour, totaling 1-6/10 (1.6) miles, begins by exit-
  ing (East) onto Genesee. Turn left (North) and continue
  to La Jolla Village Drive. Go left (West) to Regents Road
  and turn left. Continue South to Nobel Drive. Go left
  (East) on Nobel to Cargill Avenue on the right. (It is
  Costa Verde on the left.) Turn right (South) and follow
  Cargill to Decora, left (East) on Decora to Genesee, then
  left (North) to the point of beginning.

Mall Walking in San Diego County

University City

Marketplace In University City

Description: A medium-size full-service community shopping
center and post office near a primitive canyon area.
Located at 3320 Governor Road, San Diego, 92122.
Community/Area name: University City.
Thomas Guide: Page 44, Grid D-4.
Intersection of Regents Road and Governor Road.
Transit service via SDT #5, #105.   Information from 233-3004.
Typical business hours: 0800 to 2200 +/-.
Security patrol: Unknown.
Public Rest Rooms: No.   Benches: Yes.
Restaurants: There is a dining house and several sources for
snack lunches.
Walks and distances: A walk around the central building com-
plex totals 7/10th (.7) of a mile.
An up/down area walk of 1-1/10th (1.1) miles begins on Governor
Road. Go left (East) to Stetson Avenue, walk left (North)
until you reach Mercer Street. Turn left (North) on Mer-
cer to Millikin Avenue, go left to Regents Road and turn
left (uphill) to Governor. Walk left to the beginning.
There is a primitive area at the end of Regents Road.

Mall Walking in San Diego County

University Towne Centre   **University City**

Description: A very large facility with top-quality department
       stores, boutique retailers, variety restaurants, theatres
       and parklike access walks. Garage and area parking.
Located at 4545 La Jolla Village Drive, San Diego, 92122.
Community/Area name: University City.
Thomas Guide: Page 44, Grid E-2.
Intersection of La Jolla Village Drive and Genesee Avenue.
Parking entry from La Jolla Village Drive, Genesee Avenue or
       Towne Centre Drive.
Transit service via SDT #30, #34, #34A, #41, #50, #105, #150.
       Information from 233-3004.
       Also NCTD #301. Information from 722- or 743-6283.
Typical business hours: 0700 to 2200 +/-.
Security patrol: Yes.
Public Rest Rooms: Inquire for location.   Benches: Yes.
Restaurants: A wide selection of various price levels.
Walks and distances: The building perimeter walk is about 1-3/8
       (1.4) miles depending on route followed.
A 2-1/3 (2.3) miles area walk begins by exiting West onto
       Genesee. Walk left (South) to Nobel Drive, turn left
       (East) and continue to Towne Centre Drive. There, turn
       left (North) and walk to La Jolla Village Drive, go left
       (West) to Genesee. Continue left (South) to beginning.
       This is a lovely residential and town-house district.

Mall Walking in San Diego County

Vista

Description: A center for household services and furnishings.
Located at 1960 Hacienda Drive, Vista, 92083.
Community/Area name: Vista.
Thomas Guide: Page 14, Grid E-1.
Intersections of Hacienda Drive and Via Centre.
Transit service nearby via NCTD #311.
      Information from 722- or 743-6283.
Typical business hours: 0900 to 1800 +/-.
Security patrol: Unknown.
Public Rest Rooms: No.   Benches: No.
Restaurants: Several in adjoining centers at each end.
Walks and distances: The store-front sidewalk is 1/4 (.25) mile.
      A walk around the building perimeter is 6/10th (.6) mile.
Area walking is not recommended due to incomplete street and
      sidewalk construction.

Mall Walking in San Diego County

Index

The National Organization of Mallwalkers (NOMW) may be reached at P.O. Box 191, Hermann, MO 65041.

Mall Walking in San Diego County